Co-Teaching with Robots

Balancing Humanity and AI in Education

Jacob Lauritzen, EdD

GILA VALLEY PRESS

Title of the Book: Co-Teaching with Robots: Balancing Humanity and AI in Education

Author: Jacob Lauritzen

Publisher: Gila Valley Press

gilavalleypress.com

ISBN: 979-8-3492-3538-2

Co-Teaching with Robots

Contents

Technology Doesn't Teach Students

This book is about how to balance your humanity as a teacher while incorporating AI in education. It is not a laundry list of everything that AI can do. It is not a sales pitch to get on the bandwagon or be left behind.

This book is a pep talk to keep humanity at the center of the classroom even as AI begins to assist teachers in their roles. Yes, AI will be able to do many things to lighten the load for teachers. It can write lesson plans, develop curriculum, grade assignments, and provide feedback. It is hard to imagine everything that AI will be able to do in the future.

Regardless of these advancements and changes, the purpose of education is still to teach people. And as people teaching people, we can't lose sight of the heart of the classroom--a talented and trained human teacher.

It is a harsh reality that too many teachers are pushed beyond their means. This is no fault of the teachers themselves, but due to their circumstances. They have been tasked with overcrowded classrooms and underfunded budgets. They must teach students who want to be there in the same room as students who don't. They need to take students who don't speak the same language and teach them alongside students who are years behind in their development.

Teachers have always been superhuman. With the promise of AI, they have a new sidekick to help them focus on what they do best—teach.

Before I became a college professor, I spent over a decade teaching high school English. We were a Title 1 school where 100% of our students received a free or reduced lunch. Over 90% of my students were minorities. My students dealt with many challenges inside and outside of the classroom. I was always looking for the best practices to help them.

When I decided to earn a doctorate, I wrote my dissertation on how to use an adaptive computer-based reading program to improve my students' reading levels. I learned a lot about education and technology, and one fact stood out above all others:

Technology doesn't teach students.

Researchers have consistently found that putting a computer or any other piece of technology into a classroom has zero impact on learning (Timotheou et al, 2022; Carstens et al., 2021; Higgins et al., 2012). But using that equipment effectively can have amazing results.

That's where I am coming from as I approach this topic.

Technology such as AI can free teachers to focus on facilitating learning rather than completing clerical responsibilities. It can help to scale the impact of the human in the classroom while also providing valuable data to direct that teacher's efforts. It can adapt to the needs of students and provide life-changing accessibility.

Imagine for a second what that would be like:

> Students enter a classroom where they are met by their teacher. After getting settled, the teacher begins her lesson. She is free to move about in the classroom to observe her students, to adapt to their reactions, and to reteach as necessary.
>
> As they begin to work on an assignment, she roams around the room to monitor their work. She guides their practice and provides directed feedback.
>
> Before they leave, she checks their understanding through a simple exit ticket.

If the scene I described sounded like a normal classroom, that's because it should. Through research and years of developing our craft, we've learned how to teach students. Introducing AI into the classroom doesn't change that, but it does provide some new possibilities.

Instead of being stuck at her desk grading papers, taking roll, designing assignments, or writing lesson plans, our hypothetical teacher was available to "be" with her students.

And we know that there is no substitute for one on one, face to face time between a teacher and her student.

There may not be an actual robot standing at the front of the classroom with her, but with AI there kind of is. Many of the tasks that teachers may use a teacher's aid to help with, AI can do—accept of course to provide a human touch.

AI can solve so many problems, but it is still very new. We have not identified the best practices and there are many, many problems left to solve.

AI threatens the validity of test scores. It can be used to bypass learning and critical thinking. It is a cheater's best friend.

Ignoring AI doesn't serve our students though. Some have compared the significance of AI with that of the invention of the internet or even electricity. This is a historic moment. We need to adapt to this new world we find ourselves in. We need to guide our students through this transition as well.

This book is my guide to you. Like I said, I don't have all the answers, but I have learned a lot. I will share my experiences and insights. I will share what we know, and I will give some recommendations on how you can begin to incorporate AI into your classrooms.

Some of the information in this book may be outdated by the time you read it. For that reason, I won't focus too much on the specifics of current programs except to show how it can be used now and potentially in the future.

I have referenced several different AI products. Mostly I talk about Microsoft Copilot. I do that because that's the product I use most and because it is accessible to most people with an internet connection. But the principles outlined in this book can be used with many different AI products, including but not limited to OpenAI's ChatGPT, Google's Gemini, Anthropic's Claude, and more.

I am excited about AI, and I hope you are too, but if you aren't, I hope this book gives you comfort and confidence that you are not being pushed out of the classroom. You aren't going to be replaced. In fact, students need you more than ever. Technology won't ever change that.

But we do need to adapt to how education is changing. As we do that, we can solidify our place in the classroom as we learn how to co-teach with AI.

THE PROBLEM WITH ROBOTS

We Need to Be Human

"The laboring man has not leisure for a true integrity day by day; he cannot afford to sustain the manliest relations to men; his labor would be depreciated in the market. He has no time to be anything but a machine" *Walden*, Henry David Thoreau

In the fall of 2023, I attended the Artificial Intelligence Teaching and Learning Summit in Chandler, Arizona. It had been less than a year since OpenAI had released ChatGPT to the public, but the world had already changed.

This summit was one of the first of its kind. My colleagues and I attended it thinking we would see other professors from Arizona, but we quickly realized this had become a national conference. Representatives from all over the country as well as Intel and Amazon AWS were in attendance.

We didn't know what to expect. We, like many others, had been paying very close attention to what other institutions were doing about the rapid adoption of generative artificial intelligence. As an English professor, I was particularly concerned about how to address the use of AI with writing in my classroom.

My colleagues and I agreed that we couldn't stop the use of AI. It was happening whether we liked it or not.

We were hoping to find directions on what to do about it.

In the opening keynote to the conference, Anshul Sonak from Intel posed an important question: what are the skills that AI will never have?

I hadn't thought about this yet. The answer surprised me.

Human soft-skills.

AI can generate text, images, sound, even video. It can compute and analyze information. It can operate machinery, but it will never be human.

Recently, I asked the same question to Microsoft Copilot—Microsoft's generative AI assistant built on technology from OpenAI's ChatGPT. It gave a similar answer:

> **1. True Creativity:** While AI can generate art, music, and text, it lacks the genuine emotional and experiential context that fuels human creativity. The soul of creative expression is deeply personal, and that's something AI can't replicate.
>
> **2. Emotional Understanding:** AI can simulate empathy and recognize emotions, but it doesn't truly experience them. It can't feel love, joy, sorrow, or anger the way humans do.

3. **Consciousness**: AI doesn't have self-awareness or consciousness. It processes information based on algorithms and data, but it doesn't possess an inner life or subjective experience.

4. **Intuition:** Human intuition is a complex interplay of experiences, emotions, and subconscious processing. AI can analyze data and make predictions, but it can't replicate the gut feeling that comes from human intuition.

5. **Moral and Ethical Judgment:** While AI can be programmed to follow ethical guidelines, it doesn't possess an inherent sense of right and wrong. Human moral reasoning is shaped by cultural, social, and personal factors that are difficult to encode in AI.

6. **Common Sense:** AI often struggles with tasks that require common sense reasoning. It can misinterpret situations that are easily understood by humans due to their lived experiences and practical knowledge.

Throughout the conference, speakers explained that AI would impact every job and field. They reported that Morgan Stanley was predicting that 44% of the labor workforce would be affected in the next 3 years.

That was over a year ago. Change is not just coming. It is here. We, as humans, need to change our relationship with machines—and fast.

I have thought a lot about this since then.

Throughout history, advancements in technology have replaced the need for humans to perform skills and tasks. At each innovation, human labor has been replaced freeing up people to work on new problems.

I live in a small agricultural community in southeastern Arizona. Through the window of my office, I can see cotton fields. The work that used to take countless farmers to complete can be done with just one. Watering fields used to take hours to set up hoses to siphon water from ditches but now pumps and pipes can automate the process. New combines can harvest, compress, and begin the packaging of cotton for transport to the cotton gin a few miles away. Imagine the new advancements that are just over the horizon.

From that conference, I learned a very important lesson. My life as a teacher was changing. I not only need to understand the implications of AI, but I also need to learn how to use it. I would need to teach my students how to use it as well. But most importantly, I would need to develop my human soft-skills.

I would need to learn to be more human.

AI can replace almost every facet of my position, except for my human soft-skills. It will never replace my creativity, emotional understanding, consciousness, intuition, moral and ethical judgement, and common sense.

When the COVID-19 pandemic forced my students to attend class from their homes, I thought I was prepared. I was already using a learning management system. I had hundreds of videos I had already recorded on English topics. I had curriculum. But students were not prepared. Even if I had a system ready, they were not prepared to use it.

Now, years later, students tell me they prefer to take courses face to face. Many had horrible experiences with online instruction during COVID and they learned they needed to be in person—they needed a human touch.

That doesn't mean they can't benefit from online learning. They've just learned they learn better with a human in the room.

As teachers and educators, we may be apprehensive to accept the changes that AI poses. We may even feel threatened by them.

I can't tell you that you have no need to worry. Certainly, some institutions will use these advancements to replace human labor.

At the conference, they explained that those who use AI responsibly will replace those who do not. I can't predict exactly how things will play out, but this encourages me. The teachers and educators who learn how to adapt and adopt AI authentically and effectively will become more valuable, maybe even indispensable. More importantly, we will be better prepared to serve our students.

In this book, I will help you to understand the implications that AI poses for education. I will help you to understand its potential and its limitations. I will also give you practical advice on how to use AI to improve your teaching practice and to engage your students.

I can't tell you not to worry about AI, but I think we have good reason to be excited about it. I hope that by the end of this book, you'll agree that we don't have to sit back and wait for the machines to take over.

We can develop a new paradigm—one where we co-teach with AI. We can benefit from the amazing power and efficiency of AI while balancing the learning experience to provide the human touch our students desperately need.

There is still a place to be human even in an AI assisted classroom. There is still a place for you in education. I hope that by the end of this book, you'll be able to see what it is, and you'll feel empowered to accept it.

Pandora's Box

When OpenAI released ChatGPT, it unleashed a Pandora's Box of possibilities and problems. From its launch in November 2022, it quickly drew the attention of millions of people. They were excited to see how a program could write with just a simple text prompt. But this was more than a novelty.

By the end of December, over 100 million people had tested ChatGPT. It was the fastest adoption of any software program in history. I had heard about it, but I wasn't worried. Like most people, I didn't understand its potential or its power. I had no clue how it would affect me as an English teacher.

During Christmas break, I read an article about a software engineer that was trying to design a program to recognize writing written by generative AI. He wanted to make a tool to catch students that were using ChatGPT to cheat.

The article explained that although AI writing doesn't have embedded metadata to identify its source, it does follow different word patterns than human writing. Let me explain.

There are many different types of AI. ChatGPT is a form called generative AI. In short, it is designed to generate content. It is built on the back of a large language model (LLM) that has been used to train it to perform specialized tasks. In the case of ChatGPT, it had been trained on billions of texts to generate text.

As impressive as this is—and it is impressive—it doesn't work the way many people think. When you type in a prompt to ChatGPT or other AI products like it, it doesn't search for a text and give it to you. It makes a completely new text. It really does generate writing.

But it doesn't think. It doesn't even truly understand what it is writing. That's because it is based on a predictive algorithm. In other words, it doesn't take the prompt you've given it and write you something to meet your needs.

Instead, it initiates a chain reaction. It starts writing—and based on the prompt it has been given—it starts to generate a new text based on an average of its training—one word at a time.

If you have ever seen ChatGPT work, it looks like it is typing as it goes. That's because it is. It isn't a gimmick. It really doesn't know the end before it starts writing. It writes one word and then, based on its training, it writes the next most likely word using its predictive algorithm. It really is just offering an average of its training.

If you have ever seen recommended words that appear in the keyboard of your smartphone, it basically works the same way. It is trying to predict what you mean. The difference with ChatGPT is that you have given it a command to complete, and its predictions are based on that command. It is trying to predict the next most likely word until it completes its task.

I asked Microsoft Copilot if it agreed with this explanation of AI. It did, but it added the following clarification:

> **Understanding and Thinking:** While the passage correctly states that the model doesn't truly understand or think, it's important to note that it can still produce coherent and contextually relevant responses based on patterns in the data it was trained on.
>
> **Training Data:** The model's responses are influenced by the patterns and structures found in the training data, which helps it generate text that aligns with the given prompt.

Generative AI is incredibly powerful, but it is incredibly flawed. Because it writes one word at a time, it doesn't truly follow the word patterns of human writing. That's what AI checkers like the one described in the article look for. People introduce and use vocabulary at different frequencies than AI.

These checkers aren't perfect though. Turnitin.com promotes that it has a false positive rate of only 1% (Turnitin, 2024). That sounds great at first, but as someone who teaches nearly one hundred students each semester, it means that for every assignment I give, at least one of my students will be flagged for using AI when they didn't. That's a problem.

By the time I returned to class in January 2023, it became clear that I needed to understand more about ChatGPT. When I spoke to my colleagues about it, many didn't know what it was—they definitely hadn't thought about its implications on student writing.

I started to bring up AI to my students. Some were brave enough to admit that they had tried it. Others had heard about it. Most didn't know what it was.

I put it up on the projector in my classroom and modeled how it could complete one of my writing assignments—a reader response essay. We moved step by step and discussed the ethical ramifications of using it to complete an assignment. Students agreed that it felt okay to use ChatGPT to brainstorm ideas, even to outline a paper, but when we started writing a draft that felt like too much to them.

It was interesting to see their reactions. Obviously, no one wanted to own up to using it to cheat—not to their teacher—but some students were genuinely baffled at seeing what it could do. Students' jaws hung open as I worked on the problem. I showed how it could brainstorm an idea, come up with a thesis statement, outline a paper from that thesis statement, and then write an essay within a matter of seconds.

Then, I showed how I could use it to analyze the text to form an "opinion" of the text. At this point, many students started to feel uncomfortable. The power of this beta version of ChatGPT was already more than they were ready to use. That was version 3.5. OpenAI has continued to iterate and develop ChatGPT so that it is light years beyond its original capability.

Even though most students weren't trying to cheat during the first full semester it was available, I started to think how professors like me would need to adapt to this new advancement.

During the summer break of 2023, I started to update my first-year composition courses to include lessons on AI. I was hoping that by getting in front of the problem, I could model the appropriate use of AI, while also showing them that their teacher knew what was going on—that I wasn't stupid—and they shouldn't try to cheat. The reality is, it's really hard to recognize AI writing, because it looks and feels like normal writing.

As someone who reads a lot of student writing, I am pretty happy when a student can write at the level of ChatGPT, but anyone who spends a lot of time reading text written by AI might also recognize its limitations. It often feels empty. Most English teachers I've talked to about this agree, though we can't quantify it. It just feels like its missing something. Anecdotally it makes sense. Generative AI cannot produce original thought.

That's not what it's trained to do. It's designed to write an "average" text. It doesn't draw conclusions or form opinions. It presents a prediction of what others might do using the training it's been given.

It also makes mistakes. ChatGPT doesn't have access to live training data. It can't search the internet and for good reason. If it was able to constantly train itself based on the internet it could start to form a feedback loop because it could start to be trained on text written by itself or another AI product. That would corrupt the training data and cause all sorts of problems. As such, the programmers are very careful about the data being used to train the model.

This isn't the only limitation. ChatGPT can't trace back its training to a specific text. All the data is one mishmash of information. As such, it can't tell you where an answer came from. It doesn't come from a single source. It is an average of all the sources.

There is some evidence to contradict this though. In December 2023, the New York Times sued OpenAI for using its archive of articles to train ChatGPT. How did they discover this? According to the Times, they were able to ask specific questions about their content and ChatGPT could answer. It could even summarize articles. Not only had OpenAI not secured the rights to train their models using the Time's content, but anyone using ChatGPT could effectively get it for free. At this time, the lawsuit is still pending.

If a student tries to write a paper using ChatGPT, it can't cite the source of its training, because it literally doesn't know where the information came from. That won't stop it from trying though. If you ask it to provide a source, it will be happy to comply. It'll include something that looks like a citation, but because it can't identify the source of any of its training, it will be a complete fabrication. These fabrications are called hallucinations. This is one of the biggest flaws of ChatGPT as an educational product. It is an incredible tool, but it can't perform a simple task like citing a source without lying about it.

Enter Microsoft Copilot. In March of 2023, Microsoft invested 10 billion dollars into OpenAI. They were very impressed with the progress of ChatGPT, and they wanted to be able to use it in their own products. Unlike ChatGPT though, they would use its ability to read text and produce content within the context of its products. Early use of this included embedding what would later be called Copilot into Microsoft's search engine, Bing. From Bing, you could ask a question. Bing would search for the source and then Copilot would take over to search the contents of the website to produce an answer. Instead of relying on its vast database, it only had to draw from a single source to answer the question. Google's Gemini works in the same way. Because these products know where they found the information, they can identify its source—making this an invaluable tool for education.

This is only the beginning. From the early days of ChatGPT to now, Pandora's Box has been opened, and the AI race has begun. Every company has had to consider whether or not to develop their own generative AI products or build one off of the backs of services like ChatGPT.

And, as many people have often said since, this is only the beginning. This is the worst generative AI will ever be. It will only become more powerful. As educators, we need to understand that AI is not a fad. It is real and it is here. We need to learn how to adapt— and fast.

Ethical Dilemmas

The training and use of generative AI presents schools and institutions with many ethical and moral dilemmas. They need to decide if and how AI will be allowed in the classroom and what if any policy changes need to be made.

In the fall of 2023, I was asked to be on a task force at my college to figure out how we would approach the use of AI on our campus. As we began to research what others were doing, we noticed two responses.

Some colleges and universities rushed to ban and block generative AI on their campuses. They had tried to protect the academic integrity of their institution, but many found these policies were too restrictive and had to start walking back those decisions.

Other schools had taken their time. They had made small movements to protect themselves as they investigated their options.

Whether you and your institution have banned the use of AI, or you are accepting it with open arms, it is important that you adopt clear guidelines and that you communicate them to your students and faculty.

At Duke University (2025), their policy states:

> "You have the discretion to define how, if, and when generative AI may be used in your courses. However, the Duke Community Standard has been updated to include the unauthorized use of generative AI as a form of cheating."

Their guidelines continue:

> "All instructors should update their syllabi to include guidance on the use of generative AI in their class. We encourage faculty to thoughtfully consider their stance on AI use. In this shift in higher education and the rapidly changing AI market, standardized, one-size-fits-all, AI policies are not sustainable in the long term. They may also not account for the varying stances instructors will take regarding AI use in their classrooms. Furthermore, because generative AI is becoming more ubiquitous, you'll need to consider your personal stance on AI in your own work, as well as in your classrooms. Establishing an AI policy for your class allows you to have meaningful discussions with students on this topic. Being specific about how AI is or isn't allowed makes the rules clear for students and faculty if there are academic integrity violations as well."

This is what my institution chose to do.

We first looked at the policies that we already had in place. Our handbook outlined two important points on academic integrity. First, it stated that students were not allowed to turn in work that was not their own. Second, if they used work from another, they had to cite it appropriately.

We decided that these two points could be interpreted to cover the use of AI. If the work was written by AI, then it wasn't written by the student, and they couldn't submit it. Even if the student was going to acknowledge that the work was written by AI, it needed to be cited.

We also felt that it was important to let teachers decide if and how AI would be used in their classrooms.

We developed three policy statements that teachers could include into their syllabi to explain to students their rules and guidelines on AI use. They ranged from no AI, some AI, and finally to complete free rain.

Personally, I'm in the middle. I recognize that outside of my classroom, many workplaces will accept using AI to complete writing. I've used it to help me throughout the writing of this book.

But I also want my students to develop their own writing skills. So, my policy is simple: do not turn in any work that was written or includes any writing from AI.

This allows students to use AI as part of the pre-writing process, and it also avoids awkward conversations with students if their work is flagged as being written by AI.

I also have a lesson in each of my courses on the ethics of AI. It goes something like this:

We sometimes confuse three overlapping concepts: what is legal, what is moral, and what is ethical.

The legality of something is determined by the law. Governments and legislatures define what is legal, but this is not the same as what is moral or ethical. Sometimes citizens push back against the law because of these differences.

Morality is our sense of right and wrong. We may develop this from how we were raised, from our beliefs, or our experiences. Our morals can also conflict with what is legal or what is ethical.

Finally, ethics are the situational and contextual guidelines for what is acceptable. These situations can be unspoken between friends, colleagues, or they can be explicitly stated in policies.

When we talk about what is acceptable when using AI, we aren't talking about what is legal or moral. We are talking about what is ethical. As such, what might be ethical in one situation may not be ethical in another.

I then explain the rules governed by my institution and my classroom.

It is important that we explain these concepts to our students so that they understand that these rules or ethics are situational. Just because using AI is okay in one situation, it does not make it okay in all situations. One teacher may encourage it, while another forbids it altogether.

And that's okay.

We need to be clear with our students whether we approve of the use of AI and to what extent. We need to talk about it with them so that they aren't afraid to talk about it with us.

Southern Methodist University (2025) recently posted a blog post on the ethical use of AI in the classroom. The post reads:

> "As we embrace the potential of AI to enrich the learning experience, we must also confront the ethical implications that accompany its use. How can we employ AI tools while safeguarding both our values and our students' futures? What measures can we take to ensure AI aides education rather than undermines it?"

The post continues to discuss ethical concerns about misusing student data:

> "One of the biggest concerns is the handling of student data. As AI systems collect vast amounts of information to personalize

> learning, they also raise concerns about data privacy and the potential for misuse of sensitive information. Educational institutions are thus tasked with the critical responsibility of implementing data protection measures to safeguard students' personal details. Being transparent about what data collection is happening in class and how it is used could go a long way to understanding and trust in the technology. Along with that transparency, students and their guardians should also have some say over the storage of their data."

Though AI can be used to produce and analyze student data, the terms and conditions of some AI products allow them to use the data they are given to train their systems. This is potentially a FERPA violation and a huge breach of trust.

Make sure that you are aware of your institution's policies on providing student data to AI products. If your institution doesn't have a policy, you may consider adopting your own professional guidelines on the appropriate use of student data with AI.

I personally try to avoid using AI to review any identifiable student data. Because my institution pays for Microsoft's 365 service, Copilot specifically says that any data it uses is protected and not used for training purposes. Your AI products may have a similar option as well.

In my classes, I model the appropriate use and define the inappropriate use. When I discuss their writing, I have the opportunity to continue the conversation about what is acceptable or not. By the time I talk to them about their work, they have already had the concept explained to them several times. It shouldn't be new, but it may require further explanation.

Even now, with generative AI being so new, some students already find it second nature to them. They can't remember when they used AI or not, so asking them if they used it may have not even registered for them.

If we make it acceptable to at least talk about AI, then you have a foundation to continue that conversation with your students when necessary. You may need to state your policy in a syllabus, in a lesson, and even in the instructions for an assignment. You may need to do all three. Clarity is key. As AI becomes even more pervasive, it will become even more difficult to rein in.

That's why we need to constantly evolve our policies to maintain the integrity of what we do without preventing students from preparing for a world that uses AI in nearly everything they do.

I can't tell you what policies are right for you, but I do believe that we do our students a disservice to ignore AI altogether. I assume that by reading this book, you are at least open to the idea.

But as with all policies, if we are to hold our students accountable, we need to be clear on our expectations. Communicate your policies on AI to your students clearly and consistently. Don't make discussing AI taboo. Model what is appropriate or not appropriate. And be willing to change and update your policies as necessary.

The processes I outline in this book may need to be changed as the landscape of education and AI changes. We may need to even identify our policies on an assignment-by-assignment basis. Communication is key.

We may also need to communicate how and when we use AI in the development or even in the assessment of student work. Your institution may develop a policy that requires transparency, or it may simply help to build trust and confidence with students to know that you graded their work and not ChatGPT.

Many companies are starting to institute their own policies about transparency. As I publish this book through Amazon, I have had to be clear about if AI was used, to what degree, and even which programs were used.

This may be an overcorrection in the industry, or it may become the new norm. If you are an educator, you may need to consider whether to disclose how AI is being used by your institution. In time, it may become so commonplace that it is expected. Until then, we need to continue to pay attention to the needs and interests of our stakeholders so we can maintain their trust and confidence in the process.

The Interface of Artificial Intelligence

If you are new to using generative AI, there are some basics that you should understand.

First of all, generative AI is not like using a search engine. If you want to find something on Google, you type in what you want, and Google provides you with the results.

AI is different. You don't have to ask for everything at once. The AI will remember everything from your conversation, so you can provide information throughout the session. If you ask a question about something you said before, it will remember it and be able to respond accordingly. The information you give will also direct how it responds to your requests.

The more information you give the AI, the better. The results you receive are only as good as the instructions you give it, so be clear and specific.

I asked Microsoft Copilot to teach me out to use it. This was its response:

1. Starting a Conversation:

Just like you're doing now, you can start a conversation by typing a question, request, or statement. You can ask me anything from factual questions to creative prompts.

2. Asking Questions:

If you have a specific question, type it out clearly. For example:

"What's the capital of Japan?"

"Can you explain how photosynthesis works?"

3. Creative Prompts:

You can ask for creative assistance, such as writing a story, poem, or generating ideas. For example:

"Write a short story about a time-traveling cat."

"Give me some ideas for a weekend getaway."

4. Practical Tasks:

I can help with practical tasks like summarizing documents, creating to-do lists, or providing step-by-step instructions. For example:

"Summarize this article for me."

"Help me create a grocery list."

5. Conversational Engagement:

Engage in a friendly chat, share thoughts, or even ask for advice. For example:

"What's your favorite book?"

"I need advice on managing stress."

Some Tips:

Be Specific: The clearer your request, the better I can assist you.

Explore: Don't hesitate to try different types of questions or prompts. The more you explore, the more you'll discover how I can help.

Feedback: If I misunderstand or don't get it right, let me know. I aim to improve and provide the best assistance.

I like to start a conversation with AI by giving it information like who I am and what I want to accomplish. I may say something like this:

> I am a college English teacher. I want to write a letter of recommendation for one of my students.

Then I may give it context about the results I want to receive.

> The student's name is Alex Thompson. He is applying for an academic scholarship at a

> prestigious university. I taught him for two semesters, and he was a really good student.

Then I will tell the AI what to do with the information.

> Use the information I provided to write a letter of recommendation for Alex.

This is just one approach of many. You can also let the AI lead the conversation. You may say something like this:

> I am a college professor, and I would like some help writing a letter of recommendation for one of my former students. Can you help me with that?

You won't get the same result each time, but with experience you will begin to learn how to adjust your prompts to get the results you want.

Each AI has its own quirks and nuances. Some are better at some tasks than others. And they are always being updated. Don't be afraid to ask the AI for help learning what it can do and how to use it. It won't hold it against you. I promise.

Back to the Drawing Table

A few months after ChatGPT launched, I realized that I needed to rethink my priorities in my English classes.

I had always told my students that the purpose of those classes wasn't to write essays or research papers—it was to learn to think critically. The problem was I used essays to measure that critical thinking. With ChatGPT being able to produce essays, I started to wonder if there might be another way to measure my students' learning.

The first thought I, and many other teachers, had was to go analog. I could assign students one or more in-person writing assignments to either bypass AI or to get a sample for comparison purposes. This helps to maintain integrity, but it loses all of the benefits of computer-based writing.

Another thought was to incorporate other forms of assessment in addition to or in place of essay writing. This can work for many subjects, but as an English teacher this has limitations. Even if I used other assessments to measure comprehension and mastery, there was no way I was going to avoid writing completely.

For those still brave enough to require writing assignments, we can either give in to AI or try to use an AI checker. As discussed previously, AI checkers are not perfect and relying too heavily on these programs may get you and your institution into hot water. I wouldn't recommend it.

I opted to use a mixture of all of the above.

Early in the semester, I assign my students an in-class writing assignment to practice the writing process. This serves several purposes. They practice writing from an outline (as assigned), but they also give me a writing sample that I know isn't produced by AI. I can use this sample in two ways. I can compare this sample to their work as the semester progresses to see if there are any inconsistencies. I also use it to track the progress of their ideas. In other words, I can use it to get students in trouble or to help them out of trouble.

I personally don't like the role of a policeman. I became a teacher to help students—not to police them. I don't want to spend my time second guessing whether or not they've cheated on an assignment. I want to teach them.

This brings us to our second tool—AI checkers. At my institution, we are currently using Turnitin.com. As I mentioned earlier, they tout 99% accuracy—but that also means a 1% false positive or false negative rate (Turnitin, 2024). That is still too high.

I have Turnitin.com run an AI report for all the rough drafts that my students submit. If it flags a submission, then I have an opportunity to discuss it with my students before they submit their final draft. In essence, I have the opportunity to interject into the process and to show some humanity.

I typically respond with a message like this:

> "According to Turnitin.com, part of this submission was written by AI. Is this true? I will temporarily put a zero on this assignment until we have been able to discuss this."

Then the ball is in their court. When we talk about it, I have the opportunity to try to figure out if AI was used inappropriately. If everything is okay, I grade their assignment like nothing happened. If there is a problem, I may keep the zero and I've had the opportunity to address the problem.

Note that I don't call the student a liar or a cheater. I put the blame entirely on the AI checker and ask for a chance to talk to them about it.

There are many other AI checkers as well, some of which are free to teachers. Some like to use GPTZero. I personally like Scribby's Free AI Detector. You can find it here: https://www.scribbr.com/ai-detector/

I have had many different reactions to this approach. Some students will admit to using AI and we're able to have an open conversation about it. Some students choose not to talk to me at all. In that case, I leave the zero in the grade book and we move on with life. But I have also been able to identify some eye-opening situations.

I teach many international students. Some of them like to write their work in their native language and then translate it using ChatGPT. In these cases, they haven't been trying to cheat; they just wanted to use AI as an accessibility tool.

In many cases, there would be nothing wrong with this. I took the issue to my dean, and he decided that we would rather these students try to write in English than to use the tool. That gave me the opportunity to discuss the issue without, again, calling my students liars and cheaters. I just explain that in this class we're trying to get better at writing English, so we won't be using AI to translate their work.

It is important to avoid being unnecessarily punitive to our students when responding to AI. If we create barriers between us and them, we can't teach them. That ruins the entire process.

Now, I'm not saying students should be able to cheat, but we may need to reconsider how we approach assessment and respond to unauthorized use of AI. Make them learning moments—not jail sentences.

We do have a responsibility to maintain academic rigor and integrity. This is becoming more and more difficult, especially if students are willing to lie and cheat about their work. Of if they don't see an ethical problem with using AI.

Recently one of my colleagues observed that younger students didn't seem to see the problem with using AI to complete their assignments—even if it wasn't allowed.

I have observed this as well. One student couldn't remember when they did or did not use AI during the course of their work. It had already become second nature to them.

As someone older, this may seem absurd, but we witnessed the same transition with digital natives. Students who lived their whole lives with the internet—digital natives—understood the internet differently. Because they had never known anything else, they didn't have to change their thinking. They always understood it.

We are seeing a similar transition now. Younger students are becoming AI Natives. They won't remember what computing was like before generative AI and as such they will never have to make the transition. They will see its use and, yes, its ethical and moral application differently than those of us who have lived without it.

The world is changing, and it's time we learn to rethink the role of AI. So, what do we do?

Consider assessment alternatives that reinforce students' soft skills. For example, have face-to-face conversations with them about their work. This may not be feasible depending on the size of the classroom.

I schedule time into my semester to have a few conferences with my students, typically after they have submitted a rough draft.

These face-to-face conferences give me the opportunity to talk to them about their work and to address problems if necessary. It also gives them the opportunity to express their comprehension and mastery of course topics as a sort of oral quiz.

Not every form of assessment works as well with every student. More adaptation may be necessary.

In each case, we may need to reevaluate our priorities. What are we trying to teach? Is there another way to teach it? Is there another way to assess it? Are these alternatives more valid and reliable than what I am doing now?

We may need to continue to ask these questions, even if we find temporary answers to our problems. AI is going to continue to force us to re-evaluate our practices.

LESSON PLANNING WITH ROBOTS

Plan to Motivate and Engage Your Students

All the best practices for teaching and learning still apply when you use artificial intelligence.

Students can only learn what they pay attention to, and students won't pay attention if they aren't motivated. In other words, motivation leads to engagement and engagement leads to learning.

So, can AI be used to increase student motivation or student engagement?

As with most novel technology, students may be curious when they are first introduced to a new type of assignment or activity, but novelty is fleeting, and students will eventually lose interest. If we are thinking years down the road, when AI is no longer new, we won't be able to rely on it as a "shiny new object" to get their attention. We need to think more thoroughly and authentically about how it can motivate and engage students.

Let's zoom out and review what motivates students or rather what makes students unmotivated.

Confusion and Frustration

If students do not understand the purpose of an assignment or if they do not understand how to complete an assignment, they may be confused and frustrated. This frustration may eventually be too much to overcome. They will become disengaged, unmotivated, and will stop learning.

Likewise, if students do not have enough support or if they do not receive help when they ask for it, they will also be confused and frustrated.

Stress and Distractions

If students are overwhelmed or distracted by circumstances inside or outside of the classroom, they may feel the need to disengage. From the outside, this may appear as laziness or weakness. The true cause may be understood by recognizing how students are being affected by their circumstances.

Stress and distractions, no matter their source, destroy student motivation and make it very difficult to engage.

Overcoming Negative Experiences

I often tell my students that I don't know what their expectations are when they come into my classroom. If they had a bad experience in the past, I don't know it. If they don't think they're good at writing, I don't know. I just know that I am willing to help, and I believe that they can succeed. I can try to remove the obstacles I create, but sometimes I also need to learn what negative experiences they've had in the past to lead them to lose confidence in themselves.

Unfair or Unreasonable Expectations

I hate bad policies. I hate when rules prevent students from being able to succeed—and so do students. If they perceive that a situation is unfair or that expectations are too high, they may shut down. This may also stem from a lack of confidence, but if they haven't been properly prepared for an assignment, they are likely to fail. We can tell them to sink or swim, or we can help them.

I teach English. I don't teach a field with high stakes like some of you may teach. As such, I give a lot of wiggle room where other teachers may not. If I expect a student to complete a task, I make sure that I have prepared them to do it. I try to avoid asking them to do things that I haven't taught or that they haven't reasonably been taught before coming to me. Sometimes that means I reteach concepts. Asking students to do things they aren't prepared for can cause them to feel like the class isn't fair and—again—to shut down.

Any and all of these circumstances can destroy student motivation and engagement. AI may not be able to recognize these signs and over-reliance on AI to identify learning problems may lead teachers to overlook the students in front of them. This is one of many reasons why we need to maintain perspective even as we rely more and more on AI to assist us in the classroom. A teacher who pays attention to the needs of their students and has a basic understanding of psychology and pedagogy can recognize and begin to address the concerns above.

At the beginning of COVID, many teachers were caught flat footed as they were suddenly asked to teach their students from home. Some teachers tried to replicate analog and face-to-face practices that did not translate well to any form of online learning.

Regardless of pedagogy, many students felt all energy and motivation slip away. No amount of Zoom calls or emails or even the perfect online system could help them overcome the depression that overcame so many. They needed to be in person with their peers. They needed the accountability that they felt by being in the same room as their teacher.

When they lost that, they lost their motivation.

Now, that isn't to say that students are always motivated in person. Anyone with any teaching experience knows this isn't true. I'm saying that it is hard to quantify the power of a teacher seeing a student and genuinely asking them if they need help. Sometimes students just need to be with another human.

So, how can we balance the benefits of human presence with AI assisted learning? Can AI help us to recognize unmotivated students? Can it help us to motivate and to engage them?

Yes, but the same way that any tool can help. They can be used to identify motivation and engagement killers and to provide support. How? Here are some examples.

Measuring Student Motivation

Researchers have identified valid and reliable measures for both motivation and engagement. They're actually very simple.

Student motivation can be measured by surveying students. Motivation can't be reliably measured by watching someone or paying attention to what they do.

A student may seem unmotivated, but it isn't a reliable system of measurement. We have to ask our students to find out. This can be done through a simple survey.

Here is an example:

Student Motivation Survey

Instructions:

Please read each statement carefully and circle the number that best describes how true each statement is for you. Use the following scale:

1. **Strongly Disagree**
2. **Disagree**
3. **Neutral**
4. **Agree**
5. **Strongly Agree**

Survey Statements:

1. I am excited about the subjects we are studying in school. 1 2 3 4 5
2. I look forward to going to school every day. 1 2 3 4 5
3. I feel proud when I do well in my schoolwork. 1 2 3 4 5
4. I try to learn as much as I can, even when it's difficult. 1 2 3 4 5
5. I enjoy participating in classroom activities and discussions. 1 2 3 4 5
6. I believe that my effort in school will help me achieve my future goals. 1 2 3 4 5
7. I complete my homework and assignments on time. 1 2 3 4 5
8. I feel confident in my ability to succeed in school. 1 2 3 4 5
9. I ask for help when I don't understand something in class. 1 2 3 4 5
10. I feel a sense of accomplishment when I learn something new. 1 2 3 4 5

Scoring:

> Add up the scores for each statement. Higher total scores indicate higher levels of motivation.

Students can be given a simple survey like this on an ongoing basis to measure their motivation over time. AI can be used to both administer and to analyze the results from these surveys. It may be able to recognize patterns that emerge. As with all data, the more variables the more complicated and more specific the results will be.

You might find a correlation between a student dropping in motivation scores at the same time they had a significant change in their lives such as the loss of a loved one or the ending of a relationship. AI may not have all the variables to recognize these patterns (and you probably don't want to give it some of these details anyway), but if you develop a relationship with your students you may be able to connect the dots when the AI draws your attention to a pattern. In other words, the AI may notify you that a student has become less motivated over time. As you think about it, you may realize what the cause may be.

Measuring Student Engagement

Student engagement, on the other hand, can be measured by observing students. Like motivation, this can also be measured over time using a survey, but instead of asking students to complete the survey, teachers can use a survey themselves.

Here is an example:

Student Engagement Survey

Instructions:

Please read each statement carefully and circle the number that best describes how true each statement is for you. Use the following scale:

1. **Strongly Disagree**
2. **Disagree**
3. **Neutral**
4. **Agree**
5. **Strongly Agree**

Survey Statements:

1. I pay attention during class lessons. 1 2 3 4 5
2. I actively participate in class discussions. 1 2 3 4 5
3. I ask questions when I do not understand the material. 1 2 3 4 5
4. I complete my assignments on time. 1 2 3 4 5

5. I enjoy working on group projects with my classmates. 1 2 3 4 5
6. I find the class material interesting and engaging. 1 2 3 4 5
7. I take notes and review them regularly. 1 2 3 4 5
8. I feel comfortable sharing my ideas in class. 1 2 3 4 5
9. I stay focused during class activities. 1 2 3 4 5
10. I put in effort to do well in this class. 1 2 3 4 5

Scoring:

Add up the scores for each statement. Higher total scores indicate higher levels of student engagement.

You can keep track of these results in a database such as a spreadsheet and use AI to recognize patterns. Just like with motivation, you can track changes in student engagement overtime to see if there are correlations to what you are doing inside and their lives outside of the classroom. Naturally, the more variables that are involved the more complicated it is to identify causation. In short, it's really hard to prove anything unless you can control everything—which simply isn't possible. That being said, we can use AI to collect and to analyze survey data to help us as we build relationships with our students.

Clarity

As stated above, there are many factors that can destroy student motivation. You may be able to use AI to address these concerns specifically.

For example, AI can write a text or rephrase a text to make it more understandable to students. You can do this yourself or teach students how to ask AI to rephrase text for them. This gives them the tools to improve clarity in a task or a reading assignment.

Of course, this may require some oversight to make sure that students aren't being misdirected.

Focus

Many students struggle to focus. Whether this is due to a diagnosable condition such as ADHD or a lack of motivation, you can use AI to plan engaging activities or provide feedback.

Some students may need more attention than a teacher can give or constant redirection to keep them on task. An adaptive and responsive AI might be able to address some of these needs. Students can have a conversation with AI about a lesson. They can even provide tutoring. This helps to provide another source of instruction that can scale the impact and reach of the teacher.

My son likes to have conversations with his Amazon Echo. Once when he asked a question that he wasn't quite mature enough to understand, he threatened to ask Alexa. We addressed the topic, but the takeaway is illustrative. He knew where he could go to get answers—even in spite of his dad.

Sometimes we walk past his room to overhear him having conversations. He may not know it, but he is becoming an AI Native.

Positive Interactions

Students are willing to overcome difficult tasks if they are motivated enough. I often think about challenging computer games and the time students are willing to spend to beat them. They didn't stop playing because it was hard, they kept going because it was worth the effort to them.

If our students have positive learning experiences, it can help to build their intrinsic motivation to learn. Even when concepts are difficult, they can be resilient. As students learn how to engage with learning content, perhaps AI assisted content, they may feel empowered to take charge of their own learning. They can go down the proverbial rabbit holes and explore their curiosity like *Alice in Wonderland.*

Safeguards should always be in place, especially for younger students, but limiting their access to learning or framing it as bad can teach students the wrong lesson.

As they become empowered through positive learning experiences, they will learn how to become independent learners. And curious independent learners are unstoppable.

Reasonable Expectations

In addition to rephrasing content to a student's level, AI can also provide support throughout an activity. This may help students feel confident in their ability to complete a task—even if it is difficult. Students aren't afraid to do hard things, but they may feel a teacher asks too much if it doesn't seem fair or if they feel it is beyond their capacity.

AI can help to plan scaffolding, provide feedback, and other kinds of support as mentioned above.

None of these accommodations and modifications happen automatically though. It requires deliberate planning and intervention on our part. If we are thoughtful about these needs, we can anticipate and plan for these supports. In the future, some of these things may become automated—they may even be available now—but, as stated above, technology doesn't improve student learning. Good application of technology can though.

Sample Strategies for Motivating and Engaging Students with AI

Here are some strategies for motivating and engaging students with AI provided by Microsoft Copilot:

Personalized Learning: AI tools can adapt to individual students' learning styles and paces, offering tailored content and feedback. This helps students feel more connected to their learning journey.

Gamification: Incorporating game-like elements, such as challenges, rewards, and leaderboards, can make learning more engaging and fun. AI can track progress and provide real-time updates to keep students motivated.

Interactive Experiences: AI-powered technologies like virtual reality (VR) and augmented reality (AR) can create immersive learning environments. For example, students can explore historical sites or conduct virtual science experiments.

Collaborative Learning: AI can facilitate group projects by matching students with similar interests or complementary skills. It can also provide tools for effective communication and collaboration.

Real-World Applications: AI can connect classroom learning to real-world scenarios. For instance, students can use AI to analyze data for a science project or create AI-driven solutions for community challenges.

Feedback and Support: AI can provide instant feedback on assignments and offer additional resources for improvement. This helps students stay on track and feel supported in their learning.

Some of these strategies will be discussed in greater detail later in this book.

Adapt to Your Students' Needs

Despite advancements in technology, education hasn't changed very much over the years. The Socratic style of instruction where a teacher leads a group of students through a series of questions has existed for thousands of years. The "Sage on the Stage" that stands in front of a group and explains a concept is likewise a very old model for direct instruction.

Some of these strategies are still used today, because they work. But some of our traditions were born out of necessity.

When the idea of public education first spread across America, the workforce needed students who could serve the needs of industry. Today, some of our students may go into manufacturing, but others will go into the STEM fields of science, technology, engineering, and mathematics. Others may go into the arts. The model of one-size-fits-all standards and strategies doesn't serve the unique needs of our students. We need to be more adaptable.

Differentiated instruction is a model of instruction where teachers adapt instruction to meet the individual needs of their students.

Adaptation may include:

- Content: What students learn or how they learn it.
- Process: How students engage with course content.
- Product: How students demonstrate their mastery of concepts.
- Environment: How the classroom is designed to meet different learning styles and needs.

Instead of planning for one mode of instruction, one mode of assessment, and one static learning environment, differentiation suggests that teachers consider adapting how students engage with content, process, products, and environments. Not only does research support these practices, but some state and federal laws may even require modification and accommodation based on student needs.

Teachers with large class sizes and busy schedules frankly don't have time to plan differentiation. They may want to serve all the needs of their students, but time and resources prevent it.

When I was teaching high school, I tried to create a system of activities that allowed students to choose how they wanted to engage with content. In theory, it would allow my students to work at different paces, pick the activities they worked on, while still having to complete a series of lessons to show mastery for each standard. It was ambitious and I never finished it. At its heart, it was a form of differentiated instruction as a system.

It wasn't until later that I realized I was trying my own version of Universal Design for Learning (UDL). UDL is an educational framework that is accessible, adaptive, and inclusive. It can be overwhelming to implement, but research supports its practices (Ismailov & Chiu, 2022; Roski et al., 2021; Evmenova, 2018).

AI could have helped me to complete my project. Now, it can help all of us to find creative ways to adapt how we teach and how we assess our students' learning. It can't give you more time, but it can make it easier to plan for a variety of instructional and assessment strategies.

For example, let's say you want to find a few creative ways to teach a certain concept or standard. You may begin the lesson with direct instruction to the whole class, then quickly break out into different activities for guided practice. AI can help to plan and develop these activities. Consider using a prompt such as this:

> I am an elementary teacher teaching my fifth graders how to divide fractions. I'd like three different engaging activities that help my students to interact with the concept in a variety of ways. Can you help me with that?

This can start the conversation for you to develop those activities. In my experience, these sorts of conversations with AI remind me of concepts that I've learned, but don't remember at the time I am trying to make a new assignment. By "talking it out" with the AI, I can direct it to make a series of activities I could have done on my own, but that I was able to do more effectively and quickly with help.

Here is what Microsoft Copilot suggested when I used the prompt above:

1. Fraction Pizza Party

Objective: To visually understand and practice dividing fractions.

Materials: Construction paper, scissors, markers, and a worksheet with pizza recipes (e.g., "Divide 3/4 of a pizza by 1/2 to find out how many friends can share it equally").

Activity: Create pizza slices using construction paper, each slice representing a fraction.

Provide students with pizza recipes that require them to divide fractions to determine the number of slices each friend gets.

Students can cut out the slices and physically divide them among the "friends" (markers or small drawings) to see the division in action.

Engagement: Hands-on activity with visual aids to help conceptualize the division process.

2. Fraction Bingo

Objective: To reinforce the concept of dividing fractions through a fun game.

Materials: Bingo cards, fraction problems, and counters.

Activity: Create bingo cards with answers to fraction division problems (e.g., "1/2 ÷ 1/4 = 2").

Prepare a set of fraction division problems that match the answers on the bingo cards.

Call out the fraction division problems one by one.

Students solve the problems and cover the corresponding answers on their bingo cards with counters.

The first student to get a full row, column, or diagonal shouts "Bingo!" and wins.

Engagement: Combines the excitement of a game with practicing fraction division, encouraging friendly competition.

3. Fraction Story Problems

Objective: To apply the concept of dividing fractions in real-life scenarios.

Materials: Story problem cards, paper, and pencils.

Activity: Create cards with story problems that require dividing fractions (e.g., "If you have 3/4 of a pound of candy and want to divide it equally among 1/2 of a pound bags, how many bags can you fill?").

Distribute the cards to students and have them work in pairs to solve the problems.

Encourage students to illustrate their solutions and explain their thought process to the class.

Engagement: Encourages critical thinking and collaboration, making math relatable to everyday situations.

I'm not an elementary or a math teacher, but from the outside these seem like good activity-based lessons with manipulatives to engage students. They all teach and reinforce the same concept—assuming fractions have already been taught—but then they give students a variety of ways to practice and apply the lesson.

The materials also seem easy to collect. After the first year of using these (and other activities), teachers will be able to draw on them from their bag of tricks.

On a side note, I have always been impressed with elementary teachers. I have been a boring high school and English teacher. I can't imagine keeping younger students engaged all day long. What you do is amazing.

These are just a few examples of how AI can help to speed up the process of developing differentiated instruction for students. Students would have the opportunity to engage in content in a variety of ways and you, the teacher, can help to facilitate their learning as they engage in activities.

Reflect Your Students in What They Do

Before I taught college, I worked at a high school where 90% of the students were Native American. It was a wonderful experience that opened my eyes to many of my students' challenges.

Of all minority groups, Native American students have consistently scored the lowest on reading in national tests. As an English teacher, I wanted to know how I could help.

When I began my dissertation, I decided that I wanted to research how technology could be used to help my students. We were already using a reading program called Achieve3000. What made the program special was that it provided students with reading materials adapted to many different reading levels. Students would read articles adapted to their level and then, based on how well they answered questions, the program would slowly increase the difficulty of the texts.

For my dissertation, I wanted to investigate if this program could be used to help my students improve their reading levels. As I began to research, I stumbled into the concept of culturally responsive instruction.

The concept is simple: teachers intentionally provide students with content that reflects a student's culture. If that sounds familiar, it should. It is a form of differentiating instruction.

For my students, I wanted to find articles that talked about Native Americans or their culture.

At the time, Achieve3000 was unique because it had a vast library of differentiated articles. Now, AI can differentiate a text in a matter of seconds. I often model how AI programs such as Microsoft Copilot can rewrite a text to different reading levels for my college students. I explain that they can do this on their own to make a text more accessible to them.

Native American students only make up 1% of the student body in the United States. There just aren't as many Native students as other minority or majority groups. As a result, they almost never see their culture reflected in their educational materials. This isn't necessarily an oversight as it is a result of their being fewer of them. The result is the same though. They see other cultures everywhere they look, but they almost never see themselves in what they see, read, or hear.

I observed as my students often adopted other cultures. Anecdotally, they wanted to belong to something. We did our best at our school to provide opportunities for our students to express and share their culture. At pep rallies, we started to have drum circles where students and faculty could dance around a group of students chanting and drumming. We held an annual pageant where students shared their language and culture. We offered an Apache language class for students. Unfortunately, when they came into my classroom, there were few if any examples of Native stories for them to read and study. It was always someone else's "story."

So, is this a situation that AI can help with? Yes and no.

AI could absolutely rewrite a text to include the names and cultures of students, but it may not come off as authentic. Students also respond to who writes a text. I could write a story about them that highlights their cultures and practices, but it wouldn't be as meaningful as if a Native person had written it.

Rewriting a text doesn't solve that problem.

Google Gemini and Microsoft Copilot both include the ability to chat and to search. I have often used Copilot to help me research content. In the past, search engines required a lot of finesse. They could provide search results, but they couldn't search the results to answer a question—now they can.

To test his out, I went to Google Gemini and typed in this prompt:

I am looking for literature written by Native American authors past and present. Can you help me with that?

Gemini quickly provided me with a list of 14 contemporary authors and 5 past authors. It then provided me with a list of where to find their work. Subsequent questions could provide additional direction in my search. I could then use AI to help me write a lesson plan to discuss each of these works.

My classes had a minority majority, but if you have more diverse classes, you could create several assignments to reflect students' different cultures and identities. This can still take a lot of work, but with AI it is more practical than it has ever been before.

The key here isn't to adapt text for its own sake. It isn't even to be diverse to meet a standard or a quota. It is to find appropriate strategies and pedagogies to engage students. Students may increase in motivation and engagement when they see themselves reflected in the work they do. They may also benefit from seeing the world from different perspectives. AI can help to simplify and speed up forms of differentiation such as culturally responsive instruction.

Plan with AI

My first year teaching, I was working at a charter high school for at-risk youth. I was the only English teacher. I taught one class of English 9, English 10, English 11, English 12, as well as a section of Drama and a section of Creative Writing. I had six different preps and no repeat courses.

When possible, I repeated lessons across multiple classes, but that wasn't always possible. I could have benefited from an AI assistant to help me plan engaging learning activities for each of my subject areas.

I tested this out using an AI chatbot from Khan Academy called Khanmigo. Unlike ChatGPT, Microsoft Copilot, or Google Gemini, Khanmigo is a chatbot specifically trained for education.

It has been trained to help teachers create a broad spectrum of materials, including Class Newsletters, Discussion Prompts, Learning Objectives, Multiple Choice Quizzes, and more. It can level the complexity of a text, find real world context for a concept, and even customize a text for a specific need.

It's an amazing tool. When I am writing this, it is free for teachers.

So, let's work through a hypothetical situation. Let's say you are an elementary teacher, and you have to prepare several lessons, each in a different subject area. You want the content to be engaging, but not too much work to pull off.

Let's start with the Learning Objectives tool in Khanmigo.

When I open it up, it gives me the opportunity to choose a Grade Level and a Topic. After I select Fifth Grade and type in "Personal Narrative" for the topic, Khanmigo gave me the following response:

> ## Personal Narrative
>
> *Note: This tool needs your expertise to be excellent. Be sure to edit this learning objective for accuracy, clarity, and relevance!*
>
> Students will craft a personal narrative that includes a clear sequence of events, descriptive details, and a conclusion that reflects on the experience. They will also revise their narrative to enhance coherence and clarity, ensuring it meets the criteria of a well-structured story.
>
> **Student-facing objective:** By the end of this lesson, I'll be able to write a personal story with a beginning, middle, and end, using vivid details and a thoughtful conclusion. I'll also

> learn how to improve my story by making it clearer and more interesting.

Khanmigo provides me with both a teacherly learning objective that would likely look good on a lesson plan and a student-facing objective that my hypothetical students are more likely to understand.

It also puts this response into a textbox like a word processor such as Microsoft Word or Google Docs so that I can continue to revise the prompt as needed. It is also saved to "My Documents" in my Khanmigo account so I can access it later.

Let's take this learning objective to build out a lesson plan.

I copy and paste my learning objective and then go to the Lesson Plan tool. From here, I can type in a Topic and select the Format that I want the lesson plan in, and how much detail I would like Khanmigo to create.

I type in "Personal Narrative", but because it doesn't already have a lesson for that name it gives me the option to provide more information. I paste in my Learning Objective from before, and under "Notes" I explain, "I'd like an engaging activity with minimal prep and materials. Then, I select "5-Part" for a lesson plan with Objectives, Introduction, Instruction, Practice, and Assessment. I also choose "High Detail" and click "Start".

Khanmigo then produces a very detailed lesson plan with a warm-up, direct instruction guided practice, independent practice, and an exit ticket. It also provided a guide for differentiating content for students, definitions, a list of materials, and an outline for how long each part of the lesson should take.

I would copy and paste it in here, but it was over seven pages long. Simply put, it provided a very detailed plan that only required paper, a pencil, a story map template, a whiteboard, and a timer. It was exactly what I asked for.

I could repeat this process a few times and have an entire day planned very quickly. Even though, in my hypothetical situation, I needed to plan multiple preps, I was able to do it quickly within the parameters I needed.

Khanmigo currently has over 20 skills that it is trained to do to help teachers prepare and execute lessons. And this is just one AI tool. Countless companies are currently developing their own tools—perhaps with even greater power than this.

Even though Khanmigo developed the learning objective and lesson plan, it wasn't the teacher in this scenario. Students can engage directly with it like they would any other chatbot, but it still allowed for me, the hypothetical teacher, to stay at the heart of the teaching experience.

This is just one way that AI can help during the planning process. It can also make content more accessible or even create custom content.

Make Learning Accessible

A few months before ChatGPT launched, I was able to attend a virtual Open Educational Resource (OER) conference. OER's are typically free or low-cost alternatives to costly educational products. I'll talk more about these in the next chapter.

In one panel at the conference, the speakers opened my eyes to all the ways that a resource could be made accessible for students.

I hadn't fully considered how digital resources could exclude some students with disabilities. I was aware that some students with color blindness could struggle with certain colors on a screen. I knew that some students might have difficulty with seeing a text. I hadn't considered if someone could use a webpage without hands.

The panelists demonstrated how to conduct an audit for digital resources to show how they were or were not accessible. Ever since then, I have thought about how I could make my resources more accessible for students. AI is a powerful answer to the problem.

Let's imagine for a moment what an accessible classroom might look like.

It might include furniture that is easy for students of all shapes and sizes to use. Maybe it includes fidget stools for students with ADHD or chairs that can serve students of different heights and weights.

It might include microphones and speakers to amplify the teacher's voice for students who are hard of hearing. It might include clickers for students to engage with a quiz.

Maybe the colors of the room are muted to avoid being too stimulating or maybe there are soft surfaces to absorb distracting noises.

There are almost as many needs as there are students in our classrooms. How can AI help to serve these students?

In short, we need to create a learning environment that does not require students to "overcome" it. Any form of resistance can stunt student motivation and engagement, thus making learning more difficult.

Let's start with simple accessibility features.

AI can provide closed captioning. Whether on videos or during a lesson, AI can produce close captioning for audio. Students who have a hearing disability can read what they can't hear, maybe even stop and pause a video to engage with the content at their own pace.

Once a lesson is converted into text, it can also be searched. AI can produce a summary. It can even simplify the language used or rephrase it in a more accessible way. This can be done with a simple text prompt with current AI applications.

I recently had one of my students tell me that she wished she could have summaries of one of her professor's lessons because that professor talks so fast. A summary of a lesson and live captioning made using AI could prepare her for class and help her to keep up without having to ask her teacher to slow down.

If background noise is distracting, AI might be able to produce noise reduction—perhaps in the form of headphones. If the AI can isolate the audio between speakers and background noise, this could help students to focus on a speaker over other distractions.

Apple has worked on many accessibility features like this with their products. Further advances in AI could bring these services to less expensive products.

Maybe students need a text leveled to their understanding. AI can rewrite a text to a different complexity, such as a lower reading level. If students are struggling to understand a concept, AI might be able to provide an illustration, a virtual tour of a location, or even a video.

Recently, I was giving a lesson on Dorothy Wordsworth, William Wordsworth's lesser-known sister. One student joked how she wished she could just "wake" her up to ask her questions about what she had written in her journals. I opened up Microsoft Copilot and asked it to imagine it was Dorothy Wordsworth and then proceeded to ask it questions. Even now, our current AI tools can allow students to role play with deceased people or fictional characters from a story. Further advancements and we can have a virtual call with them, hearing them, and being able to engage with a virtual avatar.

Even if tools are available, students may not know that they are available or feel it is worth the hassle to use them. As teachers, we need to understand the needs of our students to know which services might serve them. We should find opportunities to model their use. Even students without disabilities can benefit from accessibility features. Students who have never been diagnosed but become aware of a solution can also benefit from a lesson modeling an accessibility feature.

A few years ago, I redesigned my online courses. As part of the redesign, I recorded nearly 100 videos explaining and modeling concepts from my classes. As part of it, I used AI to create closed captions for many of my videos. Instead of having it available in the background, I made the close captioning permanent. Even students who didn't need to see the text would have it placed in front of them.

I'm not saying that we force accessibility features onto our students, but a thoughtful inclusion of these features may serve students who don't' even know they need the help.

Create Resources with AI

In the fall of 2024, I attended the Open Education Conference in Providence, Rhode Island. This conference is a national event designed to encourage and train educators in the development of Open Educational Resources (OER).

When I got to the conference, I was surprised to find that almost half of the sessions seemed to be about the use of AI in OERs. I shouldn't have been surprised though. Generative AI enables the quick and efficient development of teaching materials such as Open Educational Resources.

Some sessions focused on basic explanations of AI, others focused on step-by-step tutorials, and a few explained the ethical and technical limitations. In one session, Dr. Dominique Scheffel-Dunand, a Professor of Linguistics at York University, discussed the problems with training AI to reflect regional dialects of languages. In short, an AI might be able to read a text in French, but could it adapt to different French-speaking regions such as Quebec, France, or Haiti. Using the wrong dialect can confuse and even offend users.

I hadn't considered this. As capable as AI is, it still has significant limitations. And yet, the problem also illustrates how far AI has come.

As I write this book, I am using Microsoft's "Read Aloud" feature built into Microsoft Word. After I select what I want to be read, I can choose which AI voice I want to listen to and how fast it reads. Not only does this help me to catch mistakes, but it also turns any text into an audio book. It's an accessibility feature that can also engage students.

As an educator, I can direct my students who would benefit from hearing a text to use Microsoft Word or any of its other products that have this feature embedded into it. This can help to address a disability or to engage them.

Because of my ADHD, I get impatient sometimes when I read. I start to skip words on the page, or I get distracted altogether. If I listen to a text, I can do something else while focusing on the words I'm reading. I've listened to this book, as well as literature for my English courses, as I go about my day, bathing my children, cooking dinner, and so on.

Consider designing an assignment where your students have to listen to a text or where they write instructions for another student who has to follow to complete a task. This scratches their brain in a new way, promotes engagement, and teaches them about accessibility.

Dr. Scheffel-Dunand also discussed some of the ethical concerns stemming from AI. As stated above, large language models (LLMs) cannot identify the source of their training. This is especially problematic in academia where citing sources is paramount to transparency. Because we cannot identify where information comes from, we cannot verify the validity of the information.

We also cannot easily identify bias in the training, and as a result, or the outcomes of materials produced by the AI.

We as educators may recognize these limitations, but we need to explain them to our students as well. If we are using AI to develop a resource, we need to verify the accuracy of the information and cite all sources as appropriate including the use of AI.

Another session at the conference promoted the use of AI to create supplementary materials for classes. This can include assignments, quizzes, readings, charts, graphs, etc. The list goes on.

As we use AI to make materials to support our instruction, we need to be transparent about when and how AI has been used throughout the process, we need to double check the accuracy of all information, and take advantage of opportunities to leverage AI to make these resources more accessible to students.

Recently, I tried an experiment. I opened up Microsoft Word on my phone and placed it at the front of my classroom. I turned on dictation and I began teaching. With few hiccups, the program was able to dictate my hour-long lecture word for word. It wasn't formatted and it wasn't pretty, but that wasn't the point.

I then took the text and uploaded it to Google's Notebook LM product. This AI technology is designed to provide a variety of methods for summarizing content. In this case, it was able to create summary notes, a FAQ, a study guide, and even an AI created podcast with two AI voices discussing the content of my lesson.

If you haven't tried Notebook LM, do it. It's amazing.

With just a few clicks, I had resources that could help my face-to-face students review what I had taught or even help my online students to participate in one of my face-to-face lessons.

It only took a few minutes to create, but the result was exponentially greater than the effort I put into it. As teachers, we are often asked to bend over backwards to serve the many needs of our students. One student is sick or out of town and they need a worksheet. Another student is gone on a sport trip and needs help catching up. A third student isn't catching on and needs the lesson explained in another way. Finding time to address all of these needs can be overwhelming.

AI can help to carry some of the load so we can keep ourselves fresh and available to help our students. It can make custom resources for one time use or to use over and over again. It can even make resources to share with other teachers.

Sample Strategies for Creating Open Educational Resources with AI

Here are some strategies for making OERs provided by Microsoft Copilot:

> **Content Generation:** AI can assist in creating educational materials like lesson plans, quizzes, and summaries. For example, generative AI tools can draft initial versions of resources, which teachers can then refine.
>
> **Translation and Localization:** AI can translate OER into multiple languages and adapt them to local contexts, making resources more accessible to diverse learners.
>
> **Accessibility Enhancements:** AI can improve the usability of OER by analyzing and addressing accessibility issues, such as providing alternative text for images or ensuring compatibility with screen readers.
>
> **Customization:** AI can tailor OER to meet the specific needs of students. For instance, it can recommend resources based on individual

learning styles or areas where students need extra support.

Collaboration and Co-Creation: AI can facilitate collaborative projects where teachers and students co-create educational content, fostering engagement and creativity.

Updating and Curating: AI can help keep OER up-to-date by identifying outdated information and suggesting relevant updates. It can also curate resources from vast repositories, saving teachers time.

Sample Prompts for Creating Open Educational Resources with AI

Here are some sample prompts for creating educational resources with AI provided by Microsoft Copilot:

Creating Lesson Plans:

"Generate a detailed lesson plan for a high school biology class on ecosystems, including activities, objectives, and assessment methods."

"Create a week-long lesson plan for middle school students about fractions, incorporating hands-on activities and digital tools."

Developing Quizzes and Assessments:

"Design a multiple-choice quiz with five questions for a university-level course on world history, focusing on the Industrial Revolution."

"Write short-answer assessment questions for a lesson on the water cycle for 5th-grade students."

Crafting Educational Content:

"Write a clear and engaging summary of the causes and effects of the French Revolution for a high school audience."

"Explain the concept of photosynthesis in simple terms suitable for elementary school students."

Enhancing Accessibility:

"Suggest ways to make this science worksheet accessible for visually impaired students."

"Generate captions for this educational video on renewable energy sources."

Interactive Activities:

"Create a classroom activity that uses role-playing to teach students about the United Nations and international diplomacy."

"Design a hands-on science experiment for a 7th-grade class to learn about chemical reactions."

Resource Customization:

"Adapt this algebra worksheet for students who are struggling with basic concepts."

"Simplify this text about the American Revolution for English language learners."

Translation and Localization:

"Translate this physics lesson plan into Spanish while maintaining the academic rigor."

"Localize this geography resource for students in South Asia."

When prompting, make sure to consider the diverse needs of your students. We will discuss more specifics on using AI for specific subjects in the next several chapters.

CO-TEACHING WITH ROBOTS

Co-Teach with AI

Throughout this book I have painted an image of robots standing side by side with teachers at the front of a classroom. Obviously, AI isn't the same as having a robot standing next to you, but figuratively that's the idea.

The future of teaching is co-teaching with AI. Sometimes that may mean taking the lead; other times, it may require stepping back and letting AI take over. The purpose of co-teaching isn't to take a break or to make your life easier—though it can do that. The purpose of co-teaching is to improve instruction through the diversity of two teachers.

In a traditional classroom, an English teacher and a history teacher may be paired together to teach a class. This system can produce synthesis that is unlikely to happen with just one teacher.

As an English teacher, I often bring history into my lessons, but I'm not a history teacher. It's not the same. When I was teaching high school, I sometimes lined up my assignments to pair with related topics being taught in my students' social studies classes. But again, that's still not the same. It can produce a united front. It may even help students make new connections, but it isn't the same as doing it together in the same room.

It can be difficult for students to see how content relates across subjects when they learn it from different teachers, in different rooms, at different times. Teaching those subjects in the same room as the co-teacher looks on can help students to see the connections.

Co-teaching also introduces diversity that students don't get from a single teacher. That diversity may be a variety of instructional strategies, perspectives, vocal patterns, and so on. That variety adds novelty that can energize a lesson or an alternative perspective that can explain an idea in a new way for students.

If we add AI into this paradigm, we can see the same potential. AI can help to provide diversity in strategies, perspective, tone, etc. It can present ways for students to engage directly with the program that also frees up the classroom teacher to work individually with other students.

The potential is incredible, but like all co-teaching relationships, it requires trust. Can we trust the AI enough to cede some of our influence and control? Can we trust that the AI will be accurate and not misleading for students?

Let's revisit the concept of hallucinations. Remember, because AI is designed to create content that mimics the work it has been trained on, sometimes it makes up content. These fabrications are called hallucinations. If students are using an AI with a closed system that cannot search for information, then the system can only provide answers based on its training data. This may lead to fabricated answers and misleading results for students.

When designing activities where students interact directly with the AI, we need to anticipate where these hallucinations may occur and to compensate for them with a system of checks and balances. That may mean a unified form of assessment that you have verified yourself. It may mean an informal assessment you conduct through conversations with the students. As with all AI, oversight is necessary.

That being said, it doesn't mean we should be afraid to lean into a co-teaching paradigm with AI in the classroom. We just need to be present enough to recognize when students need to be redirected.

It may be tempting to give too much control to AI. We can't do that either. The more disconnected we become with the process, the more detached our students will become. We cannot expect them to engage when we aren't engaged ourselves.

There is a concept in distance learning called, presence. Students need to feel the presence of other students and their teacher, especially when engaging in asynchronous learning. Otherwise, they feel like they are alone in the process. This can be addressed in distance learning by helping students to feel that a person is on the other end of the computer screen.

For my online courses, I try to send out messages to the group, respond to online forums, make custom comments on assignments, and answer emails as quickly as possible.

In a face-to-face classroom, we may take for granted that students won't face the same problem, but they can, and they will if we don't engage with them.

Several years ago, I participated in an accreditation review where I had the opportunity to go visit several classrooms at a high school. In one class, the teacher sat down at the front of the computer lab and didn't do a single thing to engage his students for the entire class period. I was baffled that not only would he do that, but that he would do that with an observer in the classroom with him. He didn't even pretend to engage with them.

The more technology we bring into the classroom, the easier it is to let technology take over. Technology itself can't teach our students. It needs to be implemented effectively with an appropriate pedagogical system. It is fine to use technology, such as AI, to assist in instruction, but students need to feel our presence.

If they see that we're looking at our phones, they may feel like they are interrupting us to ask a question. The reality may be that we are waiting for them to ask the question. Our body language is sending the wrong signal. We can combat this by showing them that we are engaged in their learning as well. Walk around, talk to them, build relationships, and make your presence known.

In the next few chapters, I will discuss specific examples for how you can co-teach with AI for different subjects starting with reading.

Read with AI

Early in my teaching career, I had the opportunity to attend a conference put on by the Arizona Department of Education. The State Superintendent of Public Instruction, John Huppenthal was the keynote speaker. I was a new teacher, and I didn't know much about his politics, but his talk stuck with me.

He said the most important skill for our students to learn was reading. As an English teacher, I appreciated this, but he also had a point. Reading is our student's gateway to the world. It is how we communicate ideas—no matter the subject area. We read in math and science as well as in the humanities. Our ability to read can give us access or it can close doors.

Around this time, I had put a simple bell work assignment on the board for my Freshmen English class. The students complained that it was too hard, and I brushed it off. I assumed that they were being lazy, and they didn't want to work. I was wrong.

Shortly after this, I gave the students in this class a reading test and I was shocked at the results. In that class, most students were reading below a 7th or 8th grade reading level. Two students were reading at a 2nd

grade reading level. One student was reading at a 1st grade reading level. When they said the bell work was too hard, they were right. I was asking them to do something they couldn't do.

As teachers, we are discouraged from giving our students assignments that they are bound to fail. We are taught strategies like scaffolding. We use accommodations and modifications and we adjust content to help our students to be successful.

I had assumed my students could handle what I felt was a simple assignment, but this group wasn't prepared for that. I could have gotten upset. I could have blamed the teachers who had taught them in the past, but that wouldn't have solved anything. They were my students now and I needed to find a way to help them. That started with improving their reading.

At the time, we were using a program that labeled all the books in the library with its corresponding reading level. Students would complete a test to measure their reading level and then I would direct them to read books in their Zone of Proximal Development (ZPD). I could then have students demonstrate their comprehension with a quiz on their book. That was the program.

It was simple and research-based, but like many programs, it couldn't do much to adapt to the needs of students. I couldn't do anything to make text more accessible. It only told them what to read or not to read.

In reading, there is a concept called, the frustration level. I love this name. The idea is simple. The longer a student spends reading content above their reading level, the more likely they are to get frustrated by it. This is called the frustration level.

It has nothing to do with their resilience or endurance. It simply acknowledges that pushing yourself beyond your limits is frustrating. It can also reinforce a student's belief that they can't succeed. In these situations, we need to provide our students with support. If we don't, they may learn the wrong lesson—that they can't do it.

As teachers, it is easy to ask our students to work harder. We know that learning requires effort. But students also need a foundation to build their knowledge. If their foundation is years behind their classmates, they may require more support than we expect.

I later measured the reading levels for several of my students' textbooks. Their Algebra 1 textbook was written at a 9th grade reading level. That seems appropriate for a 9th grade level math class, but it also meant that the average student may become frustrated reading it. In short, they didn't have a high enough reading level to use their textbooks to teach themselves.

Like Superintendent Huppenthal had said, reading is the most important subject. It is the gateway to all other subjects. If a student can't read at their level, they may struggle in all of their classes.

Can AI help with this?

I asked Microsoft Copilot and this was its response:

1. **Reading Comprehension**: I can provide summaries and explanations of texts, helping students understand complex material.

2. **Vocabulary Building**: I can define unfamiliar words and provide examples of how they are used in sentences.

3. **Practice Questions**: I can generate questions based on the text to test comprehension and retention.

4. **Reading Recommendations**: I can suggest books, articles, and other reading materials based on the student's interests and reading level.

5. **Study Guides**: I can help create study guides and outlines for reading assignments.

6. **Interactive Discussions**: I can engage in discussions about the text, encouraging critical thinking and deeper understanding.

7. **Grammar and Syntax**: I can assist with understanding grammar rules and sentence structure, which can improve overall reading and writing skills.

There is a lot that AI can do to provide support to help students to read, but it may not be intuitive for them. We can model each of these concepts for them and provide them with opportunities to practice these strategies so that when they need the support, they know how to get it—especially if we aren't available at the time.

Reading Comprehension. The first thing I show my students that AI can do is to write a summary of a text. I like to pull open a webpage or an article and then ask an AI like Copilot or Gemini to summarize it for them. I then ask it to simplify the summary to a lower reading level. This is perhaps one of the greatest features of an AI being built into a web browser. It can take any content on the internet and level it so students can understand it.

Vocabulary Building. As a student comes across a word that he or she doesn't know, AI is a very convenient solution. Not only can it define the word, but it can also explain how it's being used in the context of the passage.

Practice Questions. I'm guessing most students won't do this on their own, but it can help students create study questions they might see on a test and help them to answer them as well.

Reading Recommendations. As students become more comfortable using AI, they may enjoy asking for recommendations for reading. Students could describe the kind of text they want to find and explain why a recommendation meets or doesn't meet their expectations as well. That is much more sophisticated than the kinds of shopping recommendations at the bottom of a webpage that we're used to seeing.

Study Guides. When I was working on my master's degree, I often had to lead discussions on texts that we had read. AI can help students to come up with ideas for leading discussions, studying for tests, or simply give them an idea for what to look for in a text as they read.

Interactive Discussions. Students can simply talk to the AI about what they're reading. This is a new kind of active reading strategy that was never possible before. Instead of asking questions in their heads, students can express it to the AI and receive feedback as well.

Grammar and Syntax. Students that can articulate grammar concepts could ask AI for clarification. This may be complicated for many students, but it certainly could help a lot—especially for students who are reading in a second language.

I feel that with practice students will learn to depend on AI to help them as they read and as they study. As I think back on my experience as a student, I can see very specific ways that it would have helped me. Future versions of AI may be trained to serve this specific purpose and provide even more incredible support.

Sample Reading Prompts

You may consider planning a lesson to teach students how to use AI to help them with their reading. After guiding students through the process, you can ask them to complete this sort of activity independently or for future assignments.

Here are some sample prompts from Microsoft Copilot based on Webb's Depth of Knowledge framework (DOK).

DOK Level 1: Recall and Reproduction

1. "Summarize this text in simple terms."
2. "List three key points from this passage."
3. "Who are the main characters in this story, and what are their roles?"

DOK Level 2: Skills and Concepts

1. "What is the author's purpose in writing this text?"

2. "Describe the setting and its impact on the events in the text."

3. "Compare and contrast two characters or events in this text."

DOK Level 3: Strategic Thinking

1. "Analyze the author's use of language and its effect on the tone of the text."

2. "Evaluate the effectiveness of the arguments presented in this text."

3. "Discuss the themes of this text and how they relate to real-world issues."

DOK Level 4: Extended Thinking

1. "Rewrite a scene from this text from a different character's perspective."

2. "Create an alternative ending for this text and explain your choices."

3. "Design a project that illustrates a key concept from this text."

Write with AI

More and more I'm using AI as I write, but I'm not using it in the ways that you might think.

As I began to write this book, I thought I would try to use AI to translate my dictation into text so I could write several of these chapters by talking about them. I thought that would help me to remove some of the friction in the writing process, but I've been surprised that I haven't even tried dictation at all. At least not yet.

I'll be honest. Some of these topics in this book have been a little daunting to discuss. The thought of using AI to help build some momentum to get me through them is attractive.

I have used AI to answer some of my questions. I've used it for a few ideas. I plan on using it later to double check the accuracy of my arguments and to help me polish this before I publish it.

I haven't used it to write for me.

If you are reading this book, I imagine you've at least experimented with using AI. I can see a future where we have let down our guard and we are much more comfortable allowing AI to be used during the writing process, but for now most teachers seem to either be against it or to have some guardrails up against its use.

My current policy is that I allow AI to be used during prewriting activities such as brainstorming and outlining, but not during drafting. I also don't allow my students to use it to help revise their papers. I have no problem with AI making corrections, but I don't want an AI checker to flag their work. The more the AI rewrites, even during the revision and editing stages, the more likely it is to be flagged. I would rather avoid having to parse out which parts of a student's work are theirs or their AI's work, so I try to avoid it altogether.

Throughout this book, I have argued that we need to focus on developing human soft skills as we find balance with AI in the classroom. Where does writing fit into that paradigm?

Writing can represent our voice and our thoughts. AI can help our critical thinking, but do we want it to become the voice of our thoughts? Probably not. At least not entirely.

Developing your voice as a writer takes time. It is iterative. It is a reflection of your personality, your perspective, and your word patterns. If we begin to lean too heavily onto AI to help us to express our thoughts, we may never develop our voice.

That is a sad thought, but I am an English teacher after all.

When ChatGPT was first launched, many people began to compare it to using a calculator. They saw it as a tool to complete tasks. We also don't usually introduce students to calculators on their first day of math. We wait until they have acquired the basics before we introduce the tool to complete more complicated problems.

Maybe we should think of using generative AI the same way. But where is the line? Should we introduce it during high school? Middle school? Later elementary grades? When I posed this question to my college students, they didn't know what to say. They agreed that it was time to begin introducing calculators into math when the problems became too difficult to solve in your head. Perhaps we can use this same logic for the use of AI in student writing.

I am a college writing professor in his forties, and I feel like I am still finding my voice. I can only imagine how it might affect, maybe even stunt, that development for younger writers.

Again, I admit, I am probably placing my own values onto the problem without thinking about it objectively. But I don't think we can solve this problem without forming some opinions about it.

As our students become AI Natives, it may become clear how and when to begin teaching AI in the writing process. In leu of state standards for AI literacy, perhaps schools and districts can develop their own guiding principles for implementing AI into their classrooms.

If we use the calculator metaphor as an example, then perhaps it is time to start implementing limited AI use as students begin to conduct research.

Sample Writing Prompts

Instead of using AI to write for students, here are some sample writing prompts provided by Microsoft Copilot that students can use to help improve their writing:

Content and Structure

1. "Can you help me outline my essay to ensure it has a clear structure?"
2. "What are some ways I can strengthen my thesis statement?"
3. "Can you suggest improvements for my introduction to make it more engaging?"
4. "How can I better organize my paragraphs for better flow?"

Clarity and Style

1. "Can you help me simplify complex sentences to improve readability?"
2. "What are some ways to make my writing more concise?"

3. "Can you suggest synonyms to avoid repetition in my essay?"
4. "How can I vary my sentence structure to make my writing more interesting?"

Grammar and Mechanics

1. "Can you check my essay for grammar and punctuation errors?"
2. "Are there any spelling mistakes in my essay?"
3. "Can you help me correct any awkward phrasing?"
4. "What are some common grammar mistakes I should watch out for?"

Argument and Evidence

1. "Can you help me identify weak arguments in my essay?"
2. "What are some ways to strengthen my supporting evidence?"
3. "Can you suggest additional sources or evidence to support my claims?"
4. "How can I better explain the significance of my evidence?"

Conclusion

1. "Can you help me write a strong conclusion that summarizes my main points?"
2. "What are some ways to leave a lasting impression with my conclusion?"
3. "How can I restate my thesis in a fresh way in the conclusion?"
4. "Can you suggest a call to action or final thought for my conclusion?"

Using these sorts of prompts, model for students how to balance their relationship with AI as they write. You may consider providing a version of these or your own writing prompts aligned with a rubric or state standards. You may even assign them to seek out feedback from AI as part of their normal writing process.

Solve Problems with AI

As much as writing has been upended by generative AI, math and science subjects have also been turned completely upside down.

I honestly had no idea how to answer this question, so I asked Microsoft Copilot:

Here are a few strategies that math teachers might find helpful:

1. **Real-World Applications:** Design problems that require students to apply math concepts to real-world scenarios. This often involves multiple steps and critical thinking, making it harder for AI to generate answers without context.

2. **Show Your Work:** Require students to show their step-by-step work for each problem. This not only helps teachers see the student's thought process but also makes it difficult to simply copy answers.

3. **Personalized Problems:** Create unique problem sets for each student or group. By varying the numbers, scenarios, or parameters,

teachers can reduce the chance of students finding solutions online.

4. **Oral Explanations:** Have students explain their solutions orally or in written reflections. Understanding the reasoning behind the answer demonstrates a deeper grasp of the material.

5. **Collaborative Projects**: Encourage group work on complex problems. Collaboration fosters discussion and idea exchange, which are less likely to be completed by AI.

6. **Regular Assessments:** Frequent quizzes and in-class assignments can help ensure students stay engaged and understand the material. These can be designed to complement take-home assignments.

7. **Emphasize Understanding:** Focus on conceptual understanding rather than rote memorization. Questions that ask students to explain or explore concepts help identify genuine comprehension.

8. **Ethics Education:** Discuss the ethical implications of using AI to complete assignments. Highlight the value of honesty and personal growth through learning.

Let's take these concepts one by one.

Real World Application. This is always a good idea. Students can get all the way through school and still not understand how algebra can help them in the real world. That should never happen. Solving real world examples can address that need.

Now, can AI help with this too? Absolutely, but by providing students with a specific problem to solve and having them complete it during class, teachers will have teachable moments and an opportunity to observe how students solve the problem.

Show Your Work. This is an old strategy, but it serves multiple purposes. When students show their work, teachers have the opportunity to see how students think about the problem. It may also discourage cheating.

Personalized Problems. Students may find personalized assignments more engaging. It also makes it unusual for students to be able to find the problem solved previously on the internet. AI might still be able to guide students to the answer, but if it is more engaging, students may be more motivated to work through the problem themselves.

Oral Explanations. This is one reason why I have conferences with my students to discuss their writing. Oral explanations are a form of assessment. Not all students will be comfortable talking about their work, but it gives teachers an opportunity to talk to students about their work—literally. This may force students to expose their ignorance while also providing teachable moments.

Collaborative Projects. Project-based learning is a great form of assessment. It also creates an accountability system within the group. There will always be students who don't carry their weight within a group, but having the accountability of the group can be an effective motivator. This also gives students the opportunity to teach each other.

Regular Assessments. Measuring learning frequently gives teachers a timeline and a record of learning. This constant contact gives teachers more opportunities to recognize problems and more opportunities to provide intervention.

Emphasizing Understanding. It's very easy for students to focus on getting the "correct answer" if that's what we're measuring. If we are emphasizing understanding, it may require deeper understanding (perhaps a deeper level of knowledge), while also adding a practical perspective for the skill.

Ethics Education. I spend time every semester explaining the ethical use of AI. I explain that in some situations it is perfectly okay, while in others it shouldn't be used. I model the process, and I explain when it is okay and when it isn't within the content of my classroom. Being open and direct about appropriate use can help. You can also try to scare them into submission. I like to tell students that if they get used to using AI to bypass their own human learning now, then they won't be prepared to explain to an employer why they shouldn't also be replaced by AI. Sometimes it works.

Integrity aside, how can AI help students to learn math?

Khan Academy was founded by Sal Khan after he saw the benefit of making tutorial videos for his nephew. His background wasn't in education. He was an accountant, but he knew math and so he used his skills to help him.

The core of Khan Academy was that students could watch a video of someone working on a problem and explaining it. AI can do the same thing.

If students use AI as a tutor, they can ask it to walk them through how to complete a problem. This way, students aren't just getting an answer and passing it off as their own, they are being guided to the answer. Having learned the process, they can use it to complete future problems.

Like using a calculator, classes of the future may accept students using AI to solve problems. For the present, we still want students to learn how to solve problems practically so that we know they have the skills to do it without AI.

Sample Math Prompts

When I asked Microsoft Copilot for some sample math prompts that students can use to get help on their work, it suggested students just ask for the answer.

Naturally, AI can just solve the problem, so I rephrased the question to ask AI to help students to improve their conceptual understanding of math concepts. That got a much more useful set of prompts:

General Understanding

1. "Can you explain the concept of [specific math topic] in simple terms?"
2. "How does [specific math concept] apply in real-life situations?"
3. "What are the key principles behind [specific math topic]?"

Algebra

1. "Can you explain why we use variables in algebra?"
2. "How do linear equations represent relationships between quantities?"
3. "What is the significance of the slope and y-intercept in a linear equation?"

Geometry

1. "Why are the properties of triangles important in geometry?"
2. "How do the different types of angles relate to each other?"
3. "Can you explain the concept of congruence and similarity in shapes?"

Trigonometry

1. "What is the unit circle, and why is it important in trigonometry?"
2. "How do sine, cosine, and tangent functions relate to right triangles?"
3. "Can you explain the significance of trigonometric identities?"

Calculus

1. "What is the concept of a limit, and why is it fundamental in calculus?"
2. "How do derivatives represent rates of change?"
3. "Can you explain the relationship between differentiation and integration?"

Statistics and Probability

1. "What is the difference between descriptive and inferential statistics?"
2. "How do probability distributions help us understand random events?"
3. "Can you explain the concept of statistical significance?"

Word Problems and Applications

1. "How can I break down a word problem to understand what it's asking?"
2. "What strategies can I use to translate real-world situations into mathematical equations?"
3. "Can you explain how to identify and use relevant information in a word problem?"

If these prompts are too advanced for your students, consider revising them to be more appropriate for their level. AI can help you to do that too.

Learn with AI

If there is one best practice that the world seems to agree on, it is that anything written by AI should be double checked by a human for accuracy. This is especially true when it comes to research.

Chatbots often warn users that they should always double check results for accuracy. This is because AI can hallucinate sometimes. That being said, AI can be a fantastic tool for researching topics.

As I have written this book, I have often asked AI for specific ideas. I am already familiar with these concepts, but the AI has reminded me of topics I could include in my chapters.

How could this be used for students? In addition to guiding research as students write, AI can also help students to complete lab activities.

I am no scientist, but I had the privilege of working with Dr. Nathan Cline, a biology professor, for several AI trainings with the faculty at our institution. Dr. Nathan Cline explained how he used and developed several activities for students to complete laboratory assignments using ChatGPT.

He gave me his permission to include this lab sequence. He calls it, "Exploring Nature through the Scientific Method."

The purposes of the activity are as follows:

> 1. Understand the steps of the scientific method.
>
> 2. Make and record outdoor observations.
>
> 3. Formulate hypotheses.
>
> 4. Design and conduct simple experiments.
>
> 5. Analyze data and draw conclusions.

Students just need a way to write down their observations and access to a chatbot like ChatGPT.

After watching videos on the scientific method and how to use ChatGPT, students are ready to begin.

They are directed to use the following prompt:

> Hello AI! I am in an introductory science class and need help understanding the scientific method. My instructor would like you to walk me through the process. I want to understand the meaning of Observations, Hypotheses, Experiments, and Conclusions. Prompt me through these steps and ask me questions to help me understand the process. For example, you may ask me to take a few minutes and make observations of the natural world around me. Then ask me to make a hypothesis as to why one of those observations might be. Then, ask me to come up with a possible experiment

> to test the hypothesis. Let me know, to ask me for some simulated data and to help with the analysis of that data. Finally, ask me to draw conclusions based on my results. Through each step provide example AI prompts if needed. Consider that I have the following background [provide specific demographic data that the students wishes to share. Example - I grew up in intercity Atlanta, but I'm taking this class in Rural AZ).

The prompt is detailed. It gives AI context and a task to complete. The conversation that follows is the activity.

Students are then asked to copy and paste the text from their conversation with the AI to submit.

I have seen him demonstrate this activity several times as we've presented to our faculty and at conferences. It is amazing to see how different subjects are using AI.

As an English teacher, I had no clue what a lab even was. That's the benefit of looking beyond our own skill set to see how others are using the product to influence our own use.

We can plan activities like Dr. Cline to engage students in a conversation with the AI, we can teach them how to use AI to conduct research, or we can use it as a reference as we model research for them. The possibilities are endless.

Now think about the different types of tasks we've reviewed over the past several chapters. We've discussed using AI for reading, writing, math, and even research.

In each of these cases, the AI can be used to engage with the students in a conversation about the topic or to aid in completing a task. It can be used to make content more accessible and understandable.

If used in a face-to-face environment, it can be used to engage students as the teacher monitors and directs their attention to students who need their help.

These aren't new concepts. The real difference here is the AI's ability to take previous concepts further. Instead of a search engine, AI is a search engine that can look deeper, with context, and pull-out information. Instead of a spell checker, AI can read a text and provide feedback.

The list goes on.

The question becomes how we can use these tools to enrich what we already do. Can it help us focus on facilitating learning rather than giving direct instruction? Can it help provide one-on-one tutoring when we aren't available? Can it level content to their understanding?

As we think about the authentic application of these concepts, we will see how to apply AI in practical ways.

Not as a novelty, but as an extension of our praxis. It can further our efforts without being a distraction. It can help us focus more on doing what only we can do—be the human in the classroom—while it super charges our efforts.

And this is only the beginning.

TESTING WITH ROBOTS

Assess Student Learning

Shortly after I started teaching high school, I was told that our state had adopted the Common Core State Standards and that I needed to start learning them.

Even though there has been some controversy of these standards throughout the years, I loved what I saw in the English Standards. There was an emphasis on not just the "what" but the "why" in a text. Students were asked to understand and explain why an author used the strategy he or she did.

As the standards took effect, I had the task of designing my curriculum to prepare my students to be assessed on those standards.

I didn't know it at the time, but I was being asked to perform a type of Backwards Design. The concept, first developed by Grant Wiggins and Jay McTighe, is simple, but often overlooked.

In Backwards Design, the teacher begins with a learning objective (perhaps based on a state or course objective) and then designs assessments and instructions to accomplish that objective. In other words, they start from the back and work their way forward. Make sense, right?

In this, or any other system, it becomes important to develop and use valid and reliable assessments to measure student learning. A good assessment can provide valuable information to inform teachers about how their students are learning and where they are struggling.

You may consider a series of formative and summative assessments. Formative assessments are checkpoints in the learning process designed to measure student progress as they learn. These may include informal discussions with students, quizzes, and other lower stakes assessments. These can lead to summative assessments at the end of the learning sequence. Summative assessments, as the name suggests, are assessments at the end of a sequence such as a unit or a course.

Using Backwards Design as a model, a teacher may begin with a learning objective, design a summative assessment to measure learning at the end of the unit, and then design a series of lessons, activities, and formative assessments to prepare the student to demonstrate their mastery in the summative assessment.

If you apply some of the concepts of Universal Design for Learning, you may consider developing multiple activities and assessments to provide students alternative methods for engaging with content and demonstrating their mastery.

Does that sound like a lot of work? It sounds like a lot of work to me. This is where AI can help.

Sample Prompts for Backwards Design Using AI

Here are some sample prompts you can use or adapt to develop your own units based on Backwards Design provided by Microsoft Copilot:

Step 1: Define the Learning Objectives

"Create a clear and measurable learning objective for a 10th-grade history unit on the American Civil War. The objective should focus on critical thinking and understanding key events."

"Generate learning objectives for a 6th-grade math unit on fractions that align with Common Core Standards."

Step 2: Develop the Summative Assessment

"Design a summative assessment for a high school biology unit on ecosystems. The assessment should evaluate students' ability to analyze food webs and energy flow."

"Create a summative project for a middle school language arts unit where students demonstrate understanding of literary themes in a novel of their choice."

Step 3: Plan the Learning Activities

"Suggest a series of interactive learning activities for teaching high school physics concepts like Newton's Laws of Motion."

"Design a set of engaging activities for an elementary school unit on the water cycle, including hands-on experiments and multimedia resources."

Step 4: Create Formative Assessments for the Activities

"Generate formative assessment ideas to check students' understanding of supply and demand concepts in a high school economics class."

"Propose quick, formative checks for a 5th-grade science lesson on plant life cycles."

Combining All Steps

"Help me design a full unit on Shakespeare's plays using backwards design. Include one primary learning objective, a summative assessment that involves a creative project, three learning activities (including discussions and group work), and formative assessments for each activity."

"Create a backwards-designed unit for an 8th-grade math class focused on algebra. Include learning objectives, a summative test, daily learning tasks, and quick formative assessment strategies for each lesson."

Grade with AI

I hate grading. I should honestly be grading right now. I will do just about anything before grading. Why?

For me, I think it's the finality of it. Whether you are grading formative or summative assessments, it still feels final. And students often take grading as final too.

If I could have my way, and I know I can't, I would change how grading works altogether—but that's a rant for another day.

Grading has many challenges, but it is necessary and when done well, it can improve your instruction.

It is impossible to know how well your students are doing unless you grade or assess them in some way. That assessment may be formal or informal, formative or summative.

You can measure learning through a simple conversation or through a state mandated test. It's also important for students to know how they are doing as well. Grades can direct future lessons and communicate progress to students. As much as I hate it, I know it's important.

If there is anything I would love to pass off to AI, it's grading. But is that even a good idea?

For content that has clear and objective answers, it may make sense to use AI to carry the load of grading. Like any automated grading system, AI can recognize when an answer is correct or not. But it can do more than that.

For content that is more subjective, like English, it can use criteria that you give it to grade work as well. I have given ChatGPT and other chatbots a rubric and asked it to analyze a text. It happily gives a response based on my established criteria.

The problem isn't necessarily whether AI can do it. It isn't even if AI can do it accurately. My concern is our awareness as teachers.

When you grade an assignment, you become aware of what a student did well and where they may have failed. In the case of writing, I recognize trends and habits that my students have, and I can give them direction either towards or away from those tendencies.

AI can be trained to look for just about anything. It is an incredible tool for finding patterns—that's basically all it is—but it is hard to train the sort of behavior we actually exhibit when we grade something.

I tell my students that I will never point out everything that they could change about their writing submissions.

Not only would that be a huge time commitment, but it could also be incredibly discouraging. Imagine receiving an essay back with hundreds of red marks on it. It could completely destroy your confidence in your writing. Some students may appreciate the information, while others would lose hope that they could ever write well.

I can't tell you how many students enter my classroom already defeated and I haven't even taught them a thing yet. Grading isn't just a measurement of learning, it is also teaching, encouraging, directing, inspiring, manipulating, motivating, engaging, and more. I choose what battles I want to fight when I grade, and it isn't always the same.

Some concepts like citing sources are non-negotiable for me. I always pick those battles. But other issues, like a specific argument a student is making, I may push back on, or I may leave it alone. How do you train an AI to discern which concepts an individual student needs to work on, and which issues can wait till later.

You could create criteria that you want all students to follow. You could create an individualized learning plan. But if your goal is to save time, you may not want to do any of these things.

As important as our time is, all of our decisions as teachers should be justifiable through best practices. If I want to save time because I'm overworked and stressed out, then I should save time, but the strategies

I use may not be best practices. Just because AI can save time, doesn't make it the right choice every time.

In my current practice, I try to plan opportunities for me to meet face-to-face with my students to discuss their writing. I grade their work in front of them and give them feedback directly. I may write down my comments on the computer, but I try to make it a conversation. I do this for many reasons, but one reason is because it saves me time.

Scheduling time to discuss their paper with them helps me to work grading into my schedule. Telling a student how they did is often easier for me than writing it down. But in addition to saving time, it is also more personable. It's easy for students to ignore a comment typed into a computer. They may not even see that it's there, but if you are meeting one on one with your teacher, you are more likely to listen, maybe even take notes.

To make grading more uniform, I often use rubrics. It communicates to students what they are being graded on. It also makes it easy for me to click a button that summarizes an idea.

AI can help me to develop learning objectives, activities that align with those objectives, and a rubric that effectively measures those rubrics. AI can help with that part of the grading process and give me time to use the tool it created for me.

When I first began my doctorate, my eyes were opened up to using accurate systems for measuring and analyzing data scientifically. I came from a background in the humanities. We weren't doing anything according to the scientific method. I didn't understand what valid and reliable data was, much less what to do with it.

As teachers, we may not be trained in how to create assignments that measure data in a valid or reliable way. We may be collecting grades, but the numbers we're getting may not mean what we think they mean. That takes training—training many teachers never receive.

We can use AI to create assignments that measure learning objectives, analyze growth, and make recommendations for next steps. We can use these grading systems and administer assignments to be the human face students interact with and then lean on AI to help us to create more effective activities.

Sample Prompts for Grading with AI

Here are some sample prompts for grading and providing feedback on assignments provided by Microsoft Copilot:

For General Feedback:

"Provide constructive feedback for a high school student's essay on the causes of World

War I, focusing on structure, argument strength, and evidence use."

"Analyze this lab report and identify areas for improvement in data analysis and hypothesis formulation."

For Rubric-Based Grading:

"Apply this rubric to grade a middle school book report. Criteria include comprehension, critical analysis, and creativity."

"Evaluate this persuasive essay based on the following rubric: clarity of argument, evidence used, and grammar."

For Summarized Comments:

"Summarize this science project presentation in three sentences and suggest one improvement."

"Review this poetry assignment and provide an overall comment highlighting its strengths and weaknesses."

For Ensuring Consistency:

"Compare the grading of these two assignments to ensure consistency in applying the criteria."

"Check if the feedback on these projects aligns with the standards for this grade level."

For Grammar and Writing Review:

"Assess the grammar and spelling in this research paper and point out any recurring errors."

"Review the sentence structure and tone in this creative writing piece for an 8th-grade class."

For Student-Centered Feedback:

"Draft feedback for this history essay that is encouraging and suggests clear next steps for improvement."

"Write comments for this math assignment to help a student better understand where they went wrong and how to solve similar problems."

We'll talk more about AI written feedback in the next chapter.

Provide Feedback

Technology has changed our habits and expectations in many ways. When we send a text, we expect a response. When we make a phone call, we expect someone to pick up. When we turn in an assignment, we expect it to be graded.

Our students may never read the comments we leave on their work, but they expect it to be there.

One of the first things I tried using ChatGPT for was to see if it could help me grade papers. I created a prompt based on the rubric for an essay assignment and I asked ChatGPT to analyze the quality of the essay based on the parameters I gave it.

As expected, it was able to grade the paper (though a little harshly) and even give it a score. If I wanted, I could simply copy and paste the comments from ChatGPT and move on to the next paper. It was that simple.

But is that a good idea?

Would students be disappointed to receive AI generated feedback? My initial reaction is that students would be disappointed now, but I'm not sure how they'll feel years into the future. They may even become comfortable with the idea over time.

But if we give up the role of feedback to AI, we also lose out on a teaching moment with our students. The feedback we give to our students might be the most important teaching that we do. Not only do we have the opportunity to respond directly to something they have done, but because they have done it, they are more likely to be engaged with our responses to their work. In short, it's a moment in the learning process that we are more likely to get through to our students. Do we want to give that up?

If the promise of AI for teachers is to remove some of the load, then I completely understand why some teachers would want to use AI to remove the burden of individualized feedback for students. It requires a lot of energy to produce. It's exhausting at times. Is it even worth the effort?

We already do this to a degree when we assign multiple choice tests and quizzes that can be easily graded by computer. Students don't expect feedback in these situations. Largely, we think of these moments as summative, but if we give multiple choice activities as formative assessments they could be used as teaching moments.

AI can help to analyze the data produced by these assessments and highlight trends for teachers. Teachers can then direct their feedback individually or to the group to address those trends. The data, for example, may suggest that a particular concept needs to be retaught or has been mastered. These are powerful uses of AI that can be used to direct teacher feedback to individual students, groups, or a whole class.

AI could be used to write individualized responses to students that make understanding what they did wrong or right or how they could improve accessible. It could even be tailored to sound personal, but would students believe it?

When I taught high school, I sometimes used a program called IXL. My students absolutely hated it.

The program may have changed, but at the time it could be used to quiz students on concepts aligned with state standards. For example, I could assign students to complete a quiz on a particular concept with rhetoric.

The program would then gamify the experience. Students would receive a score that gradually went up to show their mastery of the concept.

What students hated was that if they missed a question, their score would drop—a lot. This was demotivating for many students. It was the equivalent of trying to make a jump in a video game and falling several levels. Students hated trying to climb their way back up, but the theory behind the grade drop was sound. To get a

100% on their activity, students would have to show mastery over time. That meant answering questions correctly consistently.

If students missed a question, the program would try to teach them what they did wrong. These answers were stock and were the same every time a student missed a question.

But imagine if these answers were created by AI and they were adaptive to the student. That would mean that students could engage in a learning game that taught them how to win and adapted to how they performed. The idea is intriguing for sure. But how would students react?

For IXL, students hardly ever read the feedback they were given. They were more focused on improving their scores. They would even go as far as to quit before the end to avoid the possibility of missing a question. The gamification was backfiring. Students stopped engaging because they were afraid of losing. The stakes were too high—even as a game.

I don't mean to say that IXL is doing anything wrong. I'm only observing how my students responded to a computer program that had the potential to teach them with pre-written feedback.

Obviously, the entire experience is affected by the gamification of the process, but it stands to reason that students could be highly motivated by a gamified learning experience, especially if they could receive adaptive, engaging, and personalized feedback. They may respond better to a human standing next to them and walking them through a problem, but they may also be successful learning from an AI.

I imagine the best-case scenario is a mixture of the two. Perhaps IXL will add AI to their program in the future. Either way, we can use AI to provide contact when we are busy with another student, when we are at home, or when we aren't available, but we shouldn't stop providing feedback simply because AI can do it. We shouldn't disengage from the process. We can leverage how AI can help to scale our influence, but we can't back out of the process entirely. We need to stay engaged.

Where Do We Go from Here?

One of the benchmarks that many AI developers are trying to achieve is Artificial General Intelligence (AGI). When we think of AI that thinks for itself, we are basically thinking of AGI. Here is Microsoft Copilot's explanation of AGI:

> Artificial General Intelligence (AGI) refers to a type of artificial intelligence that possesses the ability to understand, learn, and apply knowledge across a wide range of tasks at a level comparable to human intelligence. Unlike narrow AI, which is designed for specific tasks (like playing chess or recognizing faces), AGI aims to perform any intellectual task that a human can do.
>
> AGI would have the capability to reason, plan, solve problems, think abstractly, comprehend complex ideas, learn quickly, and learn from experience. It represents the next frontier in AI research and development, with the potential to revolutionize various fields by providing machines with a more profound and versatile understanding of the world.

> The concept of AGI is still largely theoretical, and achieving it poses significant technical and ethical challenges. Researchers are exploring various approaches, including advanced machine learning techniques, neural networks, and cognitive architectures, to bring AGI closer to reality.

Let's imagine for a second what AGI could mean for education.

Because AGI could reason and analyze like a human, accomplishing this feat could mean using this technology to scale or offload who is completing certain tasks. If this sounds similar to what AI is doing now, that's true. The difference is that instead of completing tasks that it has been trained to complete, AGI could be more versatile. Again, in theory, it should be able to do what a human could do—save for the obvious human soft skills we've discussed throughout this book.

What could that look like?

Well, AGI could help plan customized learning plans for students based on their needs and interests. It could provide tutoring in and outside the classroom. It could help to develop curriculum and resources. It could translate and adapt content to be more accessible to students. It can make a teacher's life easier by handling administrative and clerical tasks. It could provide personalized professional development for teachers and students. It can provide services for special education students. It can mediate collaboration.

The list goes on and on.

The rapid advancement of AI is bringing the theoretical concept of AGI into view. It might even exist at this moment without our knowing it.

Even though it sparks the imagination as to what is possible, no amount of technology will replace the role of human soft skills. We may become used to communicating with AI chatbots. We may even form parasocial relationships with them. If we can develop a balance with how we use AI today, then we establish a precedent for how to continue that relationship into the future.

Yes, some businesses may lean on AGI to provide lifelong learning support. We may all end up like the characters in the Disney/PIXAR movie, *WALL-E* (2008). Everything we've ever feared about a future with AI could happen, but until it does (and I sure hope it doesn't), we still have reason to hope for the future.

Our students thrive on our attention. They appreciate the structure of a firm hand with a soft touch. If COVID-19 was any indication, we also know that many students lose motivation when left to interact with technology for their education.

Students have always had individual needs. Some may work well with an AGI tutor and others may not. Some may thrive with these advancements and others may feel like they're being left behind. The AGI may even be able to recognize this and like Baymax in Disney's *Big Hero 6* (2014), they may even try to comfort us. They might even be successful. But we have the opportunity to develop what makes us human—our soft skills. We can leverage our love for our students to help them in ways that even AGI can't compete with.

We can love them, and they can feel that love.

Let's not lose hope when there is so much hope to have. Hope—after all—is one of the most human concepts of all. Let's embrace it and share it with our students.

References

Carstens, K. J., Mallon, J. M., Bataineh, M., & Al-Bataineh, A. (2021). Effects of technology on student learning. *The Turkish Online Journal of Educational Technology, 20*(1), 105-113.

Evmenova, A. (2018). Preparing teachers to use universal design for learning to support diverse learners. *Journal of Online Learning Research, 4*

Duke Learning Innovation & Lifetime Education. (2025). *Artificial intelligence policies: Guidelines and considerations.* Duke University. Retrieved from https://lile.duke.edu/ai-and-teaching-at-duke-2/artificial-intelligence-policies-in-syllabi-guidelines-and-considerations/

Higgins, S., Xiao, Z., & Katsipataki, M. (2012). The impact of digital technology on learning: A summary for the Education Endowment Foundation. School of Education, Durham University.

Ismailov, M., & Chiu, T. K. F. (2022). Catering to inclusion and diversity with Universal Design for Learning in asynchronous online education: A self-determination theory perspective. *Frontiers in Psychology, 13*, 819884. https://doi.org/10.3389/fpsyg.2022.819884

Roski, M., Walkowiak, M., & Nehring, A. (2021). Universal design for learning: The more, the better? *Education Sciences, 11*(4), 164. https://doi.org/10.3390/educsci11040164

Southern Methodist University. (2025, January 19). *How to use AI in the classroom ethically and responsibly.* SMU Online Learning Sciences Blog. Retrieved from https://learningsciences.smu.edu/blog/how-to-use-ai-in-the-classroom

Timotheou, S. et al. (2022). Impacts of digital technologies on education and factors influencing schools' digital capacity and Transformation: A Literature Review. *Education and Information Technologies, 28*(6), pp. 6695–6726.

Turnitin. (2024). *AI writing detection model whitepaper.* Retrieved from https://go.turnitin.com/TII_AI_HE_AIWritingDetectionModel_Whitepaper_US_0924

About Jacob Lauritzen

Dr. Jacob Lauritzen is an English professor at a small community college in southeastern Arizona. Before teaching college, he was a high school English teacher. He holds degrees in E-Learning, Literature, Creative Writing, and Theatre.

He is a father, a husband, a filmmaker, and a really big nerd.

You can learn more about his work and projects at his website https://www.jacoblauritzen.com.

www.ingramcontent.com/pod-product-compliance
Lightning Source LLC
LaVergne TN
LVHW100320210926
848480LV00003B/1197